T0113681

Love,
Relationships,
And, Sometimes,
Just Letting Go

Reginald D. Smith
Founder, RU Coached

authorHOUSE®

AuthorHouse™
1663 Liberty Drive
Bloomington, IN 47403
www.authorhouse.com
Phone: 833-262-8899

Published by AuthorHouse 07/12/2022

ISBN: 978-1-6655-6133-4 (sc)
ISBN: 978-1-6655-6135-8 (e)

Library of Congress Control Number: 2022910433

Print information available on the last page.

Any people depicted in stock imagery provided by Getty Images are models, and such images are being used for illustrative purposes only. Certain stock imagery © Getty Images.

Photos by Roy Cox www.4-optic.com.

This book is printed on acid-free paper.

ABOUT THE AUTHOR

Reginald D. Smith (Coach Reg) is a professional relationship coach and a dynamic communicator who is uniquely qualified to address matters of the heart. He is the founder of RU Coached, a coaching platform that is geared toward helping individuals participate in, strengthen, and sustain healthy romantic relationships. His clients are high-achieving professional men and women who desire quality connections that honor and support their core values.

Coach Reg provides insight using emotional intelligence to create heightened awareness for his clients as they navigate the complex challenges which relationships present. What differentiates Coach Reg (he is not a counselor or therapist) is his focus on individuals, and his gift to help them to shape the destiny of an existing or new relationship.

Coaching has less to do with what happens in a relationship. It has more to do with how a person reacts and responds, rather than the relationship experience or challenge. Coach Reg also helps individuals to find joy again. Yet, when letting go is an option, he knows that his clients face a sometimes-difficult decision. Using candor, empathy, grace, and understanding, Coach Reg has made a profound difference in the lives of individuals he has coached. He created DCIDE, an objective, proven coaching model that works. The centerpiece of the model is the design of agreement and accountability into a relationship.

An insightful and innovative professional, Reginald D. Smith utilizes the components of Emotional Intelligence (a standard industry best practice) to assist clients with developing the skills to build quality romantic relationships. He has been featured on globally-syndicated podcasts, radio programs and in Platinum magazine.

CONTENTS

DEDICATION

"This book is dedicated to all individuals who desire to pursue quality relationships with those who honor and support their core values"—Coach Reg

The individuals to whom I dedicate this book love to love their partners, yet need help with being great together. I recognized several years ago that even in the best relationships, individuals may struggle to improve.

Whether you are starting a relationship, or strengthening and sustaining it, you can benefit from the guidance I provide, which is objective and based on experience.

I am an observer of people, and I want to help those who love their partners and love their relationships. With that in mind, I chose to become a relationship coach, in order to help others.

Over the years, I have helped people, who feel challenged in their relationships, to become better versions of themselves. This is dedicated to them because I have seen so many people reflect on past decisions and then realize that they could have handled themselves better. Seeing that level of emotional remorse is not fun to witness or to coach.

However, this book is an opportunity to share the wisdom of lessons learned by others, so that readers may not have to suffer similar regrets. It is my hope that this book will serve and support my readers in their relationship journeys.

My goal in writing this book is to help you find value in the insights

I provide and to explain how relationship coaching can make things even better. Please know that in my heart, I want to serve you and your partner in your relationship journey together. If you are willing to do the work, the gains will be exponentially fulfilling for you and your person. In short, you will become a relationship ROCKSTAR!

This book is also dedicated to those who have questions which they don't know how to ask their partners and who struggle to get the answers they seek.

I dedicate this book to those who wonder how to repair a relationship.

There are those of you who are not yet in a relationship, but desire to experience a fulfilling relationship now or in the future. I dedicate this book to you, as well.

Now, I invite you to enjoy the read and enjoy the ride.

PREFACE

My journey with providing relationship coaching has been full of adventure, insight, and rewards. The adventure has allowed me to meet countless individuals who want to make their new relationships work or those who have established relationships that can get better. The insight which I have gained into the nature of romantic relationships has been invaluable in guiding me to become a relationship coach who makes a difference in the lives of people who love each other. The rewards of witnessing transformations in the lives of individuals (some who are couples) who come to me for coaching have been immeasurable.

Let me tell you more. I am Coach Reg and I am the founder of RU Coached, which is a relationship coaching practice. My clients are high-achieving men and women who desire quality relationships that support and honor their core values. I encourage the discovery of solutions that foster personal development and growth. RU Coached serves individuals who are single, or are in committed relationships, and those who are divorced, among others.

I have learned, through countless conversations with these individuals, that those who desire to build more fulfilling relationships or strengthen existing ones can indeed establish better connections with their significant others.

Relationship coaching helps people to become their best selves so that they can be present, for relationship success. Relationship coaching helps people to better understand their own needs. It helps people to communicate their expectations. When challenges surface—as they always will—people learn how to navigate them well. With my toolkit of real and useful actions steps, the individuals whom I serve can start their relationship work immediately, not months or years down the road when small problems can become mountains of pain.

RU Coached, and my personal relationship coaching style, are based on three pillars. They can be posed in the form of questions. Number one, are you focused? Number two, are you purposeful? Number three, are you evolving? In this book, I share how and why the answers to these questions are pivotal in relationship success.

Why is relationship coaching work so important to me? I want people to win and be great in their relationships! The way to do that is to be self-aware and socially-aware of themselves and of their person. I want to help people foster and nurture these skills. Finding and keeping love is very important. However, at times you struggle and may even fail, especially when you are doing the same thing the way you have always done it. I want to help you learn how to respectfully interact, and to preserve and nurture love, by showing you the skills to win and be great. Do you tell your person how he or she makes you feel and why? I can help to show you how to move your feelings from the thinking level to the communication level, by sharing my insights into the situations you present.

What are some of the challenges that are impacting relationships today? Well, I believe that since the dawn of time, people have always needed to have someone to call their one and only, their true love.

In recent decades, people's lives have largely become distracted and disconnected. They can recall that at the beginning of their relationships, time was not a factor and that they made one another a priority.

Somewhere between life, work, home and other interests, love sometimes falls to the back burner, becomes less of a priority, and receives less effort than what once was there.

I often feel regretful that conversation seems to have become a lost art. In relationships, we all need to make agreements about what is expected and what will happen when those expectations are either met or not met. Yet, often, people stop having those important conversations and agreements become forgotten.

Sometimes, the communication between individuals has eroded to the point that relationship partners will even ghost one another, before anything even gets solidified. By that I mean, they don't attempt to discuss why they may not be a good fit and why it may not be the best idea to continue seeing each other. A kind goodbye and "I wish you well" never even takes place. One person may simply just disappear. Now, I do not call that adult behavior, and actually, I call it avoidance. Maybe, the person who drops everything with no explanation is afraid of being yelled at, and leaves the reason for moving on up to speculation. He or she may not have respect for his or her person. That is definitely a choice—whether to reveal one's feelings or just to bag everything with no explanation. I am saddened to say that I see too much of this behavior lately.

Another external factor that has impacted romantic relationships is the rise of technology in our lifetime. Texting, social media, and photo sharing all have their place in our society. These technologies help to get things done more efficiently. They serve a real purpose. But when partners in a relationship rely too heavily on electronic communication—and stop communicating verbally by phone or in person—then they are replacing building and nurturing a relationship with communicating by soundbites. Sadly, that is eroding many good relationships.

In my experience, I have seen that there are usually signs to the downward trend in a relationship. Is the other person taking longer to get back to a phone message when he or she initially jumped at the chance to answer the phone in the beginning? Is he or she breaking dates, forgetting commitments, or just avoiding hanging out, all together? Is the effort of one person being met or exceeded, or is that effort not being returned? Pay attention! It can be obvious from the start when subtle changes start happening, but when individuals sweep the signs under the rug, they are surprised when their partners become bored, or too busy, or outright disconnected from relationships.

Based on all of these scenarios, there has never been a time like now when people need guidance in their relationships. This book—coupled with relationship coaching—can help individuals to become more aware, create new habits, and learn the skills necessary to help them attract and keep the love which they desire.

This book is about showing up for relationships. It is about being better prepared for relationships. This book is about how to successfully participate in what is the biggest and best investment in life—the pursuit of love. I am happy to say that by learning the steps (including my model which I call DCIDE and which will be explained later in greater detail), such love is within reach.

If you are someone who cares about your person and relationship, then the information and suggestions in this book will serve as steps to a better and more fulfilling relationship. This book is intended to serve you, so that you can win and be great in your life and in your love relationship. Only you can decide how you want to craft your relationship going forward. I am here to coach you to reach that satisfying and fulfilling point in your life.

INTRODUCTION

When I say that having concern for others makes life more fulfilling, this observation may resonate with you. Although my life has been full of diverse professional and personal interests, my concern for others has been a personal passion. It is my deep concern for the welfare of others, and for their happiness and success in healthy and loving relationships, which was the impetus for me to become a relationship coach and founder of RU Coached.

I have had an interest in the happiness of others since I was a young boy, with an inquisitive mind and a curious nature. While my mom, who is a wonderful person and parent, was a big influence on the development of my compassion and insight, she and my father decided to go their separate ways when I was ten years old. While I could not understand that situation, and even experienced two divorces myself much later in my adult life, I learned countless relationship lessons about hurt and healing. Those lessons seem to resonate well with others who have had similar experiences.

I have lived through challenges and have navigated the journey of relationships to gain a richer understanding of how they work. I have learned how important it is to be present in a relationship. I now understand that you are not defined by your relationships, but there are ways to learn and practice to become more focused, purposeful and evolving.

Throughout my life's journey, people I have met along the way have told me that they find it easy to talk with me about their relationships.

I share my lessons learned, and then give them something to grow with and go with.

Because I wanted to help people to build, create or establish more emotionally gratifying relationships, I seriously considered becoming a relationship coach.

Often told by many, you have a "gift" for helping others to navigate relationship challenges, I pursued a certification in relationship coaching. Equipped with many years of relevant and relatable life experiences, I launched RU Coached to become a premier coaching platform for high-achieving individuals. Those individuals may have realized their professional ambitions, but may be looking for that special someone to call their person, to love, and to grow in a relationship that they love.

When I work with individuals, I elicit through conversation the challenges they face. What would they like to do differently? I make a vigilant effort to offer a suggestion in the form of a question. I do not tell them what they should do, but help them to conclude what changes or steps they want to take.

I am especially devoted to relationship coaching work because I know what a failure feels like, and it's no fun to experience. My devotion comes from wanting to spare others the pain of choices that can alter your life.

People ask themselves how do I survive my broken path? That's where a relationship coach comes in. If you want a healthy relationship that supports your core values, that is strong and thriving, then the insights and approaches in this book, and the notion of hiring a coach, will work for you.

People are not perfect. It is human nature to need help. As a relationship coach, I can offer additional skills, habits, and tools. Coaching can help you to be more efficient when choosing a partner, for example. No one wants to waste their time and, yes, the birth and care of a new relationship requires time.

Take this example: Two people meet on a dating website and they decide to meet in person for coffee. One person asks, "How has the dating experience been for you?" The other says, "Why do you ask me that?", defensively. Well, the person who asks the question is simply wanting to know if the other is willing to be open and sharing. It's not nosy. It's just asking purposeful questions with an intentional approach. Gathering information to make an informed decision is a "win, win." That's how a coach can help, by providing proactive steps so that you can begin to yield the fruits of a budding relationship.

My clients are people who know they struggle with interpersonal relationships, even though other areas of life are fine. They are self-aware and manage their lives, and like the rest of us, they struggle with challenges that range from small things to things that are severely impactful.

My clients are amenable to suggestions or considerations. They are willing to receive what will serve and support them in their loves and in their lives. I use my skills to hear their challenges, offer perspective, and share insight that is relatable to them.

You may ask what is the difference between a relationship coach and a counselor? Looking through my lens as a relationship coach, I help my clients to become better versions of themselves. They look inside themselves and ask, "Am I pleased with the decisions and choices in my relationships?" They may want to evolve into persons who have more confidence, or are more courageous.

If you choose to work with a relationship coach like myself, I can look at situations with an objective eye. Based upon what you share with me and what your concern is, I help to elicit the direction of the conversation and to define how I can best be of help.

On the other hand, you may want to seek a counselor or therapist if you have addiction issues like smoking, alcohol, substance abuse, eating disorders, or experience physically or verbally abusive behavior, experience phobias, suffer trauma, or anything similar to these issues.

In contrast to these clinical reasons for getting help, the reason to see a relationship coach may be to evaluate a past relationship. Maybe you want to reflect upon what worked well and what did not. Together, we can develop a plan for how to move forward in your romantic relationship journey, to help you make decisions more clearly.

We all are seeking someone who honors our core values in our relationships and we are seeking the support for what we need. Others may like us, but do we like them, too? Paying attention to mutual feelings is important, and as a relationship coach, I am the sounding board for the relationship process, whether in getting started or sustaining romantic relationships.

Are you unhappy or dissatisfied? Do you want to improve? As your coach, I can help you to share and communicate, set agreements, and establish accountability. In fact, I have developed a model to be your step-by-step guide in finding success. I will share more about this model later in this chapter and throughout the book.

Relationship coaching is transformative. It helps you to set and to realize your goals. I will check in with you regularly to ensure that your transformation is creating the changes you want and helping you to live that better version of yourself.

I find it interesting that coaching can benefit anyone and everyone. We all have relationship goals. That is a universal fact in life. With relationship coaching, you can be on your way to successful and mutually-fulfilling relationships that work for you and your person. If you care about your person and your relationship, the choice to pursue coaching will work for you, because I have witnessed such success countless times in my practice. I invite you to begin your journey with me as your coach.

This book has been written with several key topics in mind. The topics I have chosen derive from some of the most common issues and questions with which I deal in my practice.

The first topic is, "What is Good Communication?" My clients tell me, in looking back at past relationships, that they wished they had talked more with their partner. I ask them, "Talk about what," to illustrate that it is not the content of the conversation as much as it is the quality of the communication that needs work. We can talk about anything with our partners, so long as the communication is present and effective.

Regarding good communication, I encourage my clients to introduce concerns before they become problems. I suggest that they discuss concerns proactively, negotiate, set up agreements and accountability, and then move forward.

Good communication is necessary for successful and productive relationships. That is an undeniable fact and an achievable goal, with my help.

The next topic is called "Relationship Goals." In this chapter, I invite you to reflect upon your recent romantic relationship. Ask yourself, "What was good; what would I keep or leave behind; and what did we not achieve?"

If you are not currently in a romantic relationship, ask yourself how can I become the best me through my choices in the coming year and in the years ahead?

In the next chapter, called "Do You Offer What You Ask?", I discuss how many of us are quick to make requests of their persons. It is easy to ask for what you want, but it can be harder to offer to fulfill the request of the other person. It's harder to ask yourself, "What can I bring to the relationship?"

Instead of racing to attain all of the benefits of your relationship for yourself, stop and think about how much you are willing to give—and to give first before receiving. Ask yourself, "Am I willing to offer as much as I desire?" Yes, with relationship coaching, you can evolve into someone who puts their person first. Then you can reap the rich rewards of receiving back, in gratitude and appreciation from your person, and in tangible actions which meet your needs.

In the next chapter, I discuss "Turning Complaints Into Requests." How much do you dislike it when your person starts a conversation with a criticism or complaint? Think about how that would feel to you. In relationship coaching, I help to teach how to not say what is wrong up front. Instead, you can learn how to get buy in first, then present your concern in a way it can be received well. This is very important in romantic relationships, and in all relationships.

In the chapter called "Emotional Intelligence (EQ) in Love and Relationships", I discuss how to pay attention to the components of emotional intelligence. They are social awareness; self-awareness; self-management; and relationship management. One pitfall is that you can be aware of a concern, but not self-manage it. For example, if you know you can get anxious and that your thoughts can go spinning towards the worst outcome, that is your responsibility to self-manage and not the responsibility of your person. That is just one scenario of many which I come across in my practice. There are countless other examples of how emotional intelligence plays an important role in relationships. In my subsequent chapter called "Improving Emotional Intelligence," I expand and follow-up more on EQ.

"What Makes a Relationship So Hard?" is the topic of my next chapter. This section is about understanding how a relationship progresses beyond the novelty of being excited to meet someone to doing the hard work that is necessary to sustain a long-term relationship, if that is what you are seeking.

When you realize that you and your person are two different people, even with some similarities, then you may want to know how to co-exist with one another—and to thrive. For a host of reasons, this transitionary work can be hard. Depending upon the complexity of your relationship and the personalities involved, the work involved can seem daunting. As your coach, I am here to help you.

The last three chapters in the book address what happens when things are not going well. They are titled in order: "What Do I Do When My Relationship is in Trouble?"; "How Did I Miss That?"; and "The Rebound Relationship."

Throughout the book, I provide concrete examples to illustrate each topic, covering fully how to implement the tools I have developed in my practice. Remember, we are all human, and problems and concerns are expected. This book does not suggest a rigid, machine-like process. Instead, the content of this book represents a continuum of things you can learn every day to better understand the inner workings of your relationship, and how to be proactive in the choices and behaviors you show to your person.

Once you finish this book, and reflect on what you have read, you will have the skills to read the cues and signals of what is working, what is not working, and what you can improve. You love your person and love your relationship. My dedicated and experienced assistance will always be in your corner.

Chapter One

WHAT IS GOOD COMMUNICATION?

Good communication is the cornerstone of a great romantic relationship. Yet, many people who come to me for coaching have difficulty achieving the level and quality of communication which they desire.

I became interested in finding out how men and women view communication as a function of a great relationship. As I spoke with others about their experiences in relationships, I made a focused effort to listen for the biggest reasons that they shared about why their relationships failed or succeeded.

I learned that there were five things which people really care about and consider to be crucially important. Communication was number one, followed by trust, spirituality, emotional maturation, and physical and emotional intimacy.

I agree with those men and women who tell me that good communication is number one. You may wonder why communication does not come more naturally to you and to your person. After all, you try to be sensitive. You try to listen to respond. And you try to assure your person that it is safe to be vulnerable in the space between you.

However, despite your best intents, you may feel that you may fall short in your efforts, at one time or another. When challenges come along, do you wonder how to overcome them? Do you sometimes question whether the effort is worth it? How do you begin to evolve, when the communication seems so ineffective?

In order to have good communication, you need to know about problems which are surfacing and share them. Does your person share? From your point of view, express yourself genuinely and be transparent. You love your person and love your relationship. The effort and care taken to ensure that communication occurs is so important. It's also important to not run away from communication, even when it's difficult.

Additionally, it's important to be comfortable talking with your person. If you aren't, that can be an issue. There needs to be room in the relationship for sincerity and authenticity, and to be able to talk about anything.

Great communication skills are learned in life, not granted at birth. Communication first developed in childhood within your family of origin. It was modeled by your parents and your siblings. Yet, if you feel that you did not have the example or the model early in life, it is still possible to learn good communication and to be better at it. Communication may not be your strength, but when your person extends grace and understanding to you if you struggle with communication, then together, you can improve that area of the relationship. Such struggles can be acknowledged and worked through.

Yes, there are frustrations when communication breakdowns occur. You do have a choice, however. Do you lean in to repair the breakdown, or withdraw and ignore it? The perception which can be limiting is that the conversation will be uncomfortable. You may think your person should know better. In reality, your partner cannot read your mind and doesn't know automatically what is going on.

Good communication requires a willingness to share. If you have a strong level of investment in the relationship, it's worth the effort. Yes, communication may be painful, but the tendency to withdraw needs to be dealt with.

One concern is how to talk to your person when you feel angry or offended. The key is to try to ask a question about what is happening. Something to consider is to wait until you are not angry to share the offense, when cooler heads can prevail. This is so your concern does not get lost in your delivery. Your partner may not even "hear" what you are saying because your emotions are louder than your words. Check in with yourself—using your internal awareness—before you speak. It's counterproductive to lash out when you are angry, because it results in defensiveness or withdrawal on the other end. Your feelings will be overlooked when they are raw and your emotions are on fire. Try to remember the goal, which is to provide you and your person the best opportunity to be successful in that moment. I am not trying to write a script for you, just offering something to consider so that words are not spoken that could damage your relationship and be hard to recover from later.

Good communication requires specificity about the things that bother you and the things that bother your partner. If you are getting to know each other, the feedback which you may get is not always going to be something you want to hear. You can get trapped in thoughts—and frustrations—but you want the message to land, delicately. You want the frustration to dissipate when your person listens, but how do you get there?

Now, I offer more for you to consider. What parts of your relationship do you consider placing a high value on? Remember to place a high value on communication. If so, then there are ways to deliver when the time is right. Introduce the conversation so that you can find out if your person wants to repair your concern. You can start the discussion by asking, "can we Chat?"; "I miss chatting"; "I love you, but it feels like we may be slipping on some things,"; or "I want to make sure we are good."

If you are feeling like you are communicating your concerns, but nothing changes, you may be understandably frustrated. Perhaps, you can ask your person: "Do you like the results of our relationship work together?" This is being honest, it's not an attack. You are asking a question. Take careful note of the answer to your question. If he or she says yes, do actions support the answer? Only you can know if the words to the answer align with the actions.

Another trigger point in communication may come up when one person says: "We need to talk." This is a fast way to see the other person get defensive and want to run. In lieu of "We need to talk," here is something to consider. When you say, "I would like for us to discuss..." you are being inclusive and opening up a safe space to hear and to be heard. Our language needs to support that goal, not say something which leaves your partner feeling chastised or admonished.

Do you choose not to communicate or share because you worry how your concern will be received? What is that buying you? Choose you. Don't quiet your voice because you are afraid of how you are being received. When you feel offended, how do you make your person aware? This depends on your person and your relationship. These are matters of the heart and there is no one-size-fits-all approach to effective communication.

It's better that you discover if your person is "for you", and that you discover that up front in the relationship. Is he or she on your team? Is he or she your advocate, or your champion, not your competitor or your adversary? The two of you should be allies, not enemies, in order to achieve a more cohesive, loving relationship.

Another one of my observations is that individuals sometimes expect their person to absorb their thoughts and feelings like osmosis. It doesn't work that way. Your partner is not you and may not know what is going on. Take this assumption out of the equation. It's important to open a discussion about what is happening, or to ask, how do we get back on track and on the same page? If you love your person and your relationship, you can expect that he or she will consider what you are expressing.

THE RU COACHED APPROACH

Throughout the chapters in this book, I will be introducing and elaborating on scenarios which I have encountered throughout my work as a relationship coach. I share these stories—without revealing names or personal circumstances—to help illustrate the point of the chapter.

In this chapter about communication, I would like to share a story about a woman and her partner. Their relationship had progressed to the point at which the woman was invited to his mother's home for dinner, and more than occasionally. During the work week, the woman cooked meals at home for herself. As a result, she wanted to have the opportunity on the weekends to eat out at restaurants with her partner. All too often, the man would tell her they were invited to eat at his mother's house. He knew the woman's feelings, but never shared them with his mother. This caused considerable tension.

The mother prepared and cooked dinners which she wanted to serve her guests, with no input from them. During dinner, more than once, the mother asked the woman in front of her son, "What is wrong?" The son did not step up to explain that they really just wanted to make plans at a restaurant. So, the women felt unprotected and felt that she appeared to be ungrateful.

The partner was dismissive of the woman. She was questioning the relationship. Communication was breaking down quickly and she did not know what to do.

Before I share my observations and suggestions, let me explain that I have created and developed a coaching model that I apply to scenarios like this one. The model helps me to coach my clients through their relationship struggles in using a process that will work for improvement. If the client loves his or her person and loves his or her relationship, the model will help, and the effort put in will be time well-invested.

The model is called The DCIDE Coaching Model. D stands for Define or Discuss. C stands for Communicate. The letter I stands for Introduce or Initiate. D stands for Design. Finally, E stands for Execute.

The DCIDE Coaching Model provides a comprehensive approach to establishing a new relationship or strengthening an existing one. The model allows individuals to systematically address relationship concerns and acknowledgements constructively.

DCIDE facilitates building quality connections and rewards those who are willing to do the work.

Let's go through the steps, individually, as I elaborate more on what they mean.

Define or Discuss—This is where new relationships are defined and discussions about how you relate to each other are identified.

Communicate—In this step, you actively listen with the intent to understand. This is also where you and your person can hear and be heard.

Introduce or Initiate—In this step, you bring matters of concern, celebration, or acknowledgement to the attention of your person.

Design—The genesis of creating the safe space for you and your person that is free of judgment, criticism or ridicule. In this step, relationship rules are negotiated. Successfully designing a relationship provides agreement and accountability.

Execute--Each step of the model requires execution and is necessary for the model to work.

Now that I have explained the model which I apply to scenarios for which couples need help, I'd like to share some insights about how the model can truly make a difference.

The situation I described may seem daunting, but it is actually an opportunity to introduce or to initiate a conversation, which is represented by the letter I in the word DCIDE. The woman can introduce or initiate a discussion about her feelings and explain that she wants to feel more protected when she is around her partner's mother. If she first asks this question—you care about me and about us, right?—then she will more likely receive the attention from him which the conversation deserves.

In this situation, the couple should be communicating mutually so that they can get buy in from each other. Then, they can create an agreement—or design one--about how to handle the situation.

This way, they can refer back to the agreement as a reminder to each other, rather than going around in circles discussing every detail of what they think went wrong. Going back to the agreement is a clear and simple way to become centered again as a couple, and to pledge to move forward with their feelings being heard, in order to create change.

COMMONLY-ASKED QUESTIONS

In my relationship coaching work with individuals, I often receive questions from those who want to improve how they relate to their person. In this section of the chapter, I share some of those commonly-asked questions.

Q. In summary, what is good communication?

A. It is my firm belief that good communication requires patience, grace, understanding, and a willingness to learn what you don't know about the other person. Good communication results when there is a free exchange of ideas and feelings, the members of the couple are heard and understood, agreements are created, and then, they are executed well over time.

Q. Why is it so important to listen first?

A. Sometimes in relationships, individuals may find themselves competing to be heard. Communication and comprehension go hand in hand. It's important to ensure that you understand what is being said. You may have the tendency to jump ahead because you think you know what your person is saying. You need to ensure that you understand to truly reflect the other person's reality. Take the opportunity to ask a question. Tell him or her what you are hearing. Ask is that what you intended to convey? Then listen closely to the answer.

Chapter Two

RELATIONSHIP GOALS

*I*n my work as a relationship coach, I have the wonderful opportunity to meet people from all backgrounds and walks of life, many of whom are high-achieving or career-established individuals, and who come to me for coaching because they want to evolve in their personal relationships.

During the course of my work, I also have the great opportunity to do video presentations that viewers tell me they think are informative and engaging. A recent presentation about relationship goals elicited many great interactions with and responses from viewers.

I asked them questions that I posed as food for thought. One question I asked was about retrospection and review. The question was, "What have you learned about your relationship?"

Viewers were engaged and the answers were illuminating. One viewer said that she learned more about herself while in her relationship. She said that it's okay to love yourself. It's not necessary to try to fix the problems of the other person. When she realized that, she was able to become still within herself and introspective about her own role in relationships.

Another viewer realized, when looking back in her relationships, that some of those were worth maintaining because they were a blessing, while others required walking away from.

I then asked my viewers, "What is the one thing you would change about relationships, moving forward?"

One viewer said that she came to believe that her approach to her relationships should change, because she was being unrealistic. She came to understand that people are what they show themselves to be, and that it's better not to fit them into her expectations. She learned that she had a habit of trusting people too fast and that not everyone is like her.

Another question that I posed was "What is essential for building solid foundations in relationships and how do you nurture them?"

One person said that it's important to start by being honest about your beliefs, morals, and values. That way, she reasoned, she would be less likely to tolerate inappropriate behaviors, and would be more consistent. Regarding nurturing, she said that in order to cultivate a relationship, it's important to communicate daily.

I love these answers about how to reflect about relationships and how to turn that reflection into positive change that will help you to love your person and to love your relationship.

As you can probably tell, the content of this chapter is about relationship goals. When entering a new relationship or becoming introspective about an existing relationship, setting goals about your hopes for the future is a way of being intentional in your relationship. Setting goals shows that you are aware of what your person is presenting and that you have the courage to take an honest look. That is...if you are committed to your person and if you desire a high-quality relationship.

The truth is that the way in which you start a relationship is exactly what you can expect going forward in your relationship. It's important that you understand those expectations from the beginning.

There are several ways of "being" when you want to ensure relationship success.

First of all, be more reflective of what has gone well, what hasn't, what new outcomes that you would like, and know what is your clear plan to achieve them.

In the new dating scenario in which you meet someone new, think ahead early on if you can trust what you are seeing. It's important that you pay attention so that you can make an informed decision. If you don't like your outcomes, be ready to make the necessary changes.

The second strategy in setting relationship goals is to be more appreciative. Let those you love and care about know that you appreciate them and tell them why. Sometimes, we do not realize we are not sharing how we feel. Be more mindful to help you set new habits to achieve your goals.

A third strategy is to be more intentional and focused about your values and your boundaries. When you are intentional, you will be less distracted. Focus on your various relationship goals by taking them in small chunks. Ask yourself, "How do I rebuild my habits and develop new ones in support of my relationship goals?" This way, you can realize your personal wants, you can achieve them, and you can feel worthy of them. You will become stronger as a result.

A fourth approach is to be more communicative and to listen compassionately. These two approaches go hand in hand. You pay attention to what your person says. Try to decipher what he or she didn't say, which is more intangible.

Try not to rush the process. You may say to yourself, "Well, we just talked, so we're fine." Take a step further and tell your person in your own words what you heard from him or her, to validate that you listened to the meaning of the words and really "got it." Ask your person, "What's going on?" or "What is happening?" Your actions speak volumes about your interest in really knowing what's going on in his or her mind.

Next, be more patient with yourself and with others. Exercise patience, not convenience. Let me explain. You may like someone a lot, and he or she may like you back. You are both good people. However, it takes time to find out whether you both may want to stay in the same space. You may discover that your mutual space is one to continue. On the other hand, by taking time, you may eventually find out that you are really good friends, rather than lovers. In that case, you still care about that person, but you want him or her to end up in a better place romantically. It takes time to figure out what you honestly desire going forward, and to back that up with actions.

Now, try to be more determined. Be more disciplined in pursuit of your goals. New habits don't come overnight. Starting a new routine doesn't automatically happen. Habits are formed in the subconscious mind, yet you need to make a conscious choice to make them happen.

Lastly, try to be courageous enough to honor your values and boundaries, even when it is uncomfortable. It's important to protect your space. Become more familiar with what triggers you and how to respond to those triggers. Think about how to address those triggers going forward. When I coach individuals on this, they tell me that they wish to become better at producing the desired results. My suggestion? Have a game plan, and a new goal, to achieve a different outcome when you are triggered. Don't be afraid to say something, in a respectful way. Speaking up is an investment in yourself, an investment of your time and effort. When you are invested, you can look forward to the realization of your new goals by developing the skills and tools which better serve you.

So, going forward, what will you do? If you are meeting someone for the first time, try to get outside of your own mind. Do you think he or she likes you? Or is that person just being polite? You are better off not trying to read minds. Allow the conversations to unfold naturally and allow time to reveal whether interests are mutual.

If you are in an existing relationship, and the goal is to avoid repeating certain behaviors, work on starting new habits. Allow the relationship to be "breezy" as you both move towards those better outcomes. Yes, this work is hard, but try to keep it light.

Finally, I want to share a few words on confidence. Having or showing confidence is always an underlying goal to secure any relationship. Whether that new person you meet chooses you or not, stay confident in yourself. If not, thank him or her for not taking up a lot of your time. Don't come across as "thirsty." Confidence is one of those qualities that is attractive. Know that you will be okay, no matter what the outcome.

THE RU COACHED APPROACH

When it comes to relationship goals, sometimes the fundamental first step is to ask questions of your person when he or she is trying to communicate a concern to you. By that I mean to try to take the time to understand what the other person is saying before you react. In chapter one, we reviewed how important it is to listen. This is different. I am offering something else to consider. Be patient and let the other person fully explain his or her point. If you set this goal for yourself in your new or existing relationship, you will definitely see an improvement.

Let me tell you a story about someone who approached me with a problem about needing the goal in the relationship to be a patient and thorough discussion of the problem.

The couple I am referencing is now actually married. When you learn about the problem that surfaced after a short time of dating, you may be surprised. However, the point of the story is to illustrate how the DCIDE model can work to resolve a problem. In this example, I will refer to the "I" part of the DCIDE model, which stands for introduce or initiate.

When the couple was first dating, the attraction was strong for both of them. The woman, being upfront and open, was the first person to ask this important question to her partner: "Will you agree to date me exclusively?" This was certainly fair and appropriate. After all, she was expressing how she felt.

Well, her partner's answer came as quite a surprise to her. He said, "Let me think about it."

Two or three weeks passed and he said nothing else. Well, the woman was tired of waiting and was ready to throw the baby out with the bath water, so to speak.

When he finally called her back, he said, "Yes, absolutely I want to date exclusively."

She wondered, "Why did he take so long?" She asked herself, "Is his delay in answering her a bad sign?" "Could she even trust his sincerity?" she thought.

This couple could certainly have avoided a lot of anxiety and confusion if they had introduced or initiated questions for one another. When the man said, "Let me think about it," the woman could have asked, "Are you searching for someone else in your life?" She could have asked, "Do you have a concern about us going forward?"

Those questions could have been clarified as the man introduced or initiated his own point of view about his intentions. He could have answered in this way: "I care about you, but your request is so important that I want to be certain before I respond. It would not be fair to you to take this lightly."

Early on, when she felt clueless and in the dark during his delay, she could have said, "I feel bothered because you are not answering me."

She could have asked, "Why are you keeping me hanging like this?" and said, "Please help me to understand."

Out of patience and calm, the introduction or initiation of questions could have soothed many hurt feelings.

Thankfully, the relationship ended up working out and became a lifelong bond through marriage. I can only hope that the lesson learned by this couple is to set a goal in their relationship to ask questions when something is unclear or unexplained. It costs nothing to say, "I thought I understood, but I am not quite certain." The relationship goal of asking a question is to achieve clarity.

Another relationship goal illustrated by this story is to allow yourself time and grace to get to know someone slowly. Tell yourself, "Let me be patient because this person may be important to me, but I don't yet know."

The relationship goal of asking questions is important to people in existing relationships as well. Try not to become defensive when your loved one of five, ten, fifteen, or twenty years asks you a question for clarification. Indeed, it is a sign of attempting to listen and to understand better. Let me be clear. I am speaking about questions, not interrogations. The way the question is posed can be a trigger to your person and they may react in this way: "I can't believe you asked that!" At this point, it's important to invite your person to talk about how he or she got to this point of reacting, and slow down, and maybe even start over.

Another something to consider: When you say you want to talk, or to ask a question, to initiate or introduce a concern (which is what the model suggests), try not to minimize the topic of conversation. This is important if the concern is very significant. I can tell you from personal experience that introducing a serious topic by saying, "Hey, do you have a second for a quick talk?" can really go south into a tension-filled conversation when the other person is caught off guard. It can take a lot of strength for the other person to not respond defensively, or to not push back, or to avoid AAA (attack, accuse, assume).

A relationship goal can be to introduce or initiate a difficult conversation openly and sincerely, while giving the other person a true idea of what it's about. Although you may not end up in a long-term relationship like the couple in this scenario did, you can walk away satisfied and fulfilled with the conversation that starts with a question and ends with being completely understood.

COMMONLY-ASKED QUESTIONS

Q. When is it a good time to discuss the relationship goals with your person?

A. It's important to plan a time when you can feel confident and clear about what you want from the relationship, in order to share your goals. As you talk together, you are seeking to be on the same page as your person, to find out whether you want the same things in the relationship. You need to feel comfortable talking about the things that are important to both of you. Are your goals aligned? In order to get to a mutual sense of wanting to continue and to move forward, you need to consider when you are ready to be the listener and receiver of thoughts, and when your person is also ready to do the same. Take your time and don't try to rush this conversation. The outcome can be better when you are both in a receptive place.

Q. What can I do when I realize my relationship goals might not be met in the relationship?

A. There is no "one-size-fits-all" answer here. It's a decision that only you can make and it can be an emotional decision. Ask yourself, "Now that I have invested time in this relationship, am I at a crossroads?" "Is my partner not following through on the goals which we agreed to?" If the answer is yes, find the courage to move on.

There is no right or wrong here. You may actually choose to stay, but you need to be willing to accept what comes along with that. Your goals may remain unfulfilled. Consider something: Is this sustainable? If you keep your goals at the forefront of your decision, you open up the possibility that you could meet another person that's for you and who is 100 percent behind the goals you can agree on.

Chapter Three

DO YOU OFFER WHAT YOU ASK?

*D*oes it seem easier to ask for what you want from your partner than to receive and listen to what they want? For example, maybe you like to hike and would love for your person to go, and enjoy the scenery and the physical activity. Maybe you would rather stay home and watch a movie on Friday night, along with your special someone.

Most of us do not struggle with what we want, especially if we give much thought to our needs and desires. Yet, weaving in the needs and desires of your partner is essential to being great together. While a relationship coach can help to design the blueprint of how to reciprocate with your loved one, the work is really yours to carry out after coaching.

I would like to share a story to bring home the point. I play in a weekly golf league. One time, a member of the league asked me to share what I do occupationally, and I said that I am a relationship coach. As we got to know one another, I learned that he was a young, single man who told me that he noticed a shift in his dating life. He was in his early 40's. He said that he noticed that the women he dated seemed to feel that the drive and ambition of the men they dated should match theirs. In other words, he was dating high-achieving women, who wanted to date people with a similar high-achieving attitude. They seemed to have a preconceived notion about what a man should be like and were discarding men who did not fit the ideal image.

The women whom he met were setting a high expectation from the start, but in his world, what someone does for a living is not as relevant as the person's character and core values. The man wondered to himself-"What is more important, to have many possessions and date only people who are nice-looking, or to be involved in a more substantive relationship?" He decided to keep trying to meet new people, and shaped his definition of a mate as someone who supports the same values and who will complement his. His goal will take time and patience, which will be well worth the effort.

The scenario I just described shows the importance of looking for specific attributes which both individuals should be willing to offer. If you have an investment in a relationship, whether dating for a short or a long while, it's very important to check in with yourself about this question: do you offer what you ask? In the beginning, there may be a physical attraction and interesting conversation. If you decide to continue a relationship, you need to be clear about what you want. You need to expect the same from your person. Both individuals need to be in the same space about things that matter. This philosophy holds true for individuals in long-term committed relationships.

Each of you can set a standard to strive for. Inside your mind, it may be a requirement to stay engaged and committed to the relationship. In the process of communicating your standards, define those boundaries. If you know what you care about, and are seeking a confident person with a good self-image, it's also important to project the same qualities. That is offering what you ask for. It's something to consider as you carve out the path to your relationship.

However, not all smooth beginnings continue to be satisfying and reciprocal. When partners hit a brick wall and feel that a dealbreaker is happening, what do they do? Recognize and address behaviors and actions that can make relationships go south, early on.

For example, is it a dealbreaker when a woman wants a man to talk to her, but he is not a good communicator and avoids conversations? Ultimately, that is up to them. I do not have one simple recipe for success, but I can suggest that if the divide between them is deep and unresolvable, that they not settle. The stakes are too high to assume that everything will work out or that the circumstances will change. If someone shows you who they are in the beginning, believe them.

This part of the chapter brings me to the concept of taking a loss, also known as "Taking an L." Sometimes, individuals know that the person they are dating is not meeting or exceeding their needs. Perhaps one person in the relationship feels like a lower priority, but does not feel courageous enough to communicate and expect more. Perhaps, one member of the couple tends to not be truthful, and the other overlooks this behavior time and time again. His or her needs become negotiable because the relationship has become so familiar and comfortable, that the lying is tolerated. Little things become big things that should have been addressed in the beginning. With no intentions to end things, slowly the connection wastes away and the individuals wonder why they are not happy.

Another aspect of offering what you ask for involves the discovery process, when two people are first getting to know one another. If you like to ask questions to get to know him or her better, that is fine, and even necessary. When it's his or her turn to ask you questions, offer what you requested—time and attention to sharing the information. In this way, your early dating rituals will have balance, and fairness, and mutual standards.

In fact, asking questions in the beginning is like data gathering. This stage of sharing is important because as you continue to get to know him or her, and things show up that are contrary to what was presented, you can have it addressed as soon as you feel concerned.

Just saying the words, "I would like it if you (fill in the blank here)" is not enough. Pay attention and notice if your needs are being met. The same thing applies to your partner. All of this work takes time as your relationship evolves. Remember that anything worth having is worth your patience. How do you know and understand the ending to a play at the theatre if you haven't been present for all of the acts of the play? It's better not to fast forward in your relationship, just like it's better to keep your attention all the way through a performance.

Let's revisit the idea of dealbreakers, and the existence of double standards. Double standards can be dealbreakers. They happen when a person wants something of you, but will not reciprocate. It's not about "quid-pro-quo" or pettiness. Simply put, people who use double standards are not offering what they ask of you.

For example, if a woman wants her partner to date her exclusively, yet she wants to date other men, that is a clear double standard. She is not offering what she asks. He may be tempted to take a loss or "take an L", but at some point, he may question if it's worth it. He may feel that he is facing a dealbreaker.

So, if you offer what you ask, you are applying the same standards in the relationship. A dealbreaker is probably not in the making. That's the goal and the expectation, from the beginning of the relationship, onward.

On the other hand, if your budding relationship is about having fun and keeping it light, with no commitment intended, then you may or may not get to the point of agreements and expectations. But if you feel interested in something long-lasting, look for the following: equal standards, and expectations that are honored, met, and exceeded. It's important to look for someone who will offer what they ask of you. So that if you evolve to love your person and to love your relationship, you can meet each other's needs by offering what you each need, desire, and expect.

THE RU COACHED APPROACH

In this section, I would like to share a story about a man and his significant other. In this story, the man starts a relationship with a woman. Over time, the topic of spending time with friends, family and colleagues comes up. He really wants to maintain his past relationships by going to dinner or lunch or a sporting event, occasionally. He does not intend to see the woman any less or allow this to impact the time he has for their relationship. Surprisingly, though, when the woman wants to keep in touch with her old friends, he objects. He is not offering what he asks for. Does the woman slow down or stop hanging out with friends, family and colleagues, just to keep him? In addition, the man feels that he is not getting attention, and that her neutral get togethers constitute some type of threat.

This story is a good example of double standards. That's because the man wants to be free, but places his partner in a box when she wants to make choices freely. She would be wise to suggest a discussion. "How can you continue an old friendship, and tell me that I cannot do the same thing?" is a reasonable question for her to ask. Understandably, it's not fair if the man moves through the relationship as if he lives on an island with input from no one about his social life. Consideration towards the woman's needs is part of addressing the needs of the couple, because the individuals are no longer independent of one another in their relationship.

Using the RU Coached approach, let's apply the DCIDE model to this scenario. The couple should first define an open a line of communication which is non-threatening. Avoid AAA (attack, accuse assume). Then, they can introduce or initiate the challenge they are facing. Next comes the crucial step here. In this example of blending separate lives, the couple can design an agreement that helps to hold them accountable to one another. Keeping the same standard for the man and the woman is essential, which means either they trust one another to enjoy the freedom of hanging out with old friends, or they mutually agree to limit it. Whatever the choice, the couple can collaborate reasonably and execute the agreement which they have designed.

A little role playing can help to shed light on this scenario. Here it goes:

The woman: "I am not 100 percent clear. Did I miss something?"

The man: "I feel that it is okay to keep seeing an old friend, even though we need to make time for us."

The woman: "I get it, but I want to do the same."

The man: "Babe, I trust you and you trust me. Let's discuss and agree before any lunches or get-togethers even happen."

The woman: "That's fine with me, as long as I have the same freedom to see old friends."

The man: "Yes, so we agree that we each talk it over first. We both have the same freedoms."

I hope this dialogue shed some light on things. To be clear, as long as the man and woman respect and execute the agreement, they can be great together, until the next challenge comes up for discussion and agreement.

This story reminds me of the story I shared earlier about a woman who felt like her partner was not protecting her when his mother became critical. I recently heard that the man was in a car accident. He called the woman first to let her know about the accident, and the conversation ended there. Who did he actually call to drive to the accident location and offer help? He called his mother for that! His partner found out and obviously, did not like that. She wanted him to call her for comfort and help, not his mother.

The woman remembered that he called her "number one in his life", but failed to show action in that instance. The tension between them was difficult. If the tables were turned, he would expect her to call him first because he was the priority in the relationship. He was more than a boyfriend and was the first person who would come to her mind in a crisis. The double standard here was obvious.

What happened next? The couple had already invested much time and attention in the relationship. They continue to try to make decisions which are fair to each of them. Stay tuned for more on this couple.

COMMONLY-ASKED QUESTIONS

Q. I asked an important question of a guy I was dating: "Do you ever think that it's appropriate to lie?" He said absolutely not. Later, he told a lie and I found out about it. The lie was born from convenience, meaning it was easier to tell a lie than to tell the truth. I confronted him. He responded, "You asked me if lying is appropriate. I stand by that." So, how could I have asked my question differently to get the answer I needed? How can I recognize a double standard?

A. Posing a clear and accurate question is important. Here is something to consider—by asking him to repeat what he heard, in his own words, he would then have the opportunity to give a straight answer. Using a clear question that offers no wiggle room allows you to initiate a clear agreement that he would not lie. If he lies again, then he has revealed his true self. Another something to consider—if someone shows you who they are, believe them and their actions, not just their words. This situation could turn into a dealbreaker, without a doubt.

Q. What if I struggle to accept the way my person chooses to handle a situation?

A. This question addresses a common challenge in relationships. It's important to remember to respect the choices of your partner, even when you don't understand those choices. Respect them even if you do not like the choice. Respect them even when you do not agree with the choice.

Sometimes, a situation arises and how your person feels is revealed. If you take for granted how he or she feels about a given topic, you could be blindsided by those actions. You express your feelings and they dig in—no changes. Now, you have a choice to make. You ask yourself, "Do I accept the situation and love him where he is, or does the choice alter or even damage the relationship?"

Ask yourself if you are committed to the relationship. However, you want him to respect and accept your choices. Reciprocate back to him. Your blueprint for your next steps lies in the title of this chapter: "Do you offer what you ask?"

Chapter Four

TURNING COMPLAINTS INTO REQUESTS

Complaining is perhaps one of the biggest reasons for disagreement in a relationship. It can affect communication, collaboration, and even commitment in the lives of individuals and their partners.

Complaining can sound like nagging, as you know. One person with whom I work told me that when her person complains, she feels like she is hearing nails scraping across a chalkboard. Another individual with whom I once worked said that complaining can be a form of distraction from the conversation at hand, and can often be used to deflect blame or to hurt one another.

Although it is not always easy, turning complaints into requests can yield much better results for a couple who may be struggling to be understanding and supportive of each other. Before I get into an explanation about how to do this, I want to address the important question of why.

Why is it so important to turn complaints into requests? Remember from an earlier chapter in this book that constructive and productive communication is essential for success. However, in relationships, we can become complacent and even lazy with our communication. In the beginning, communication can happen easily as the two individuals are discovering one another. Even for existing couples, the feeling of being able to talk about anything may have given a spark to their relationships in the beginning.

Yet, once the novelty fades, you may become complacent and comfortable, and your relationship may be marked by subtle changes. You and your partner may even start taking each other for granted. You may show less effort, and things may start to slip.

Next, your communication may not be as deliberate. You and your person may start to speak harshly, or even blurt things out. Simple things like asking a question may be followed by a sharp and negative response, like "Why are you asking me that?"

The problem is that your communication was once loving and productive, but now it sounds like complaining. You may feel like you are hearing the same complaints over and over again. Your partner may feel the same way.

Turning complaints into requests helps take the sting out of communication that has slipped backwards. Turning complaints into requests can make your partner feel more receptive to you. Most importantly, turning complaints into requests can create a bridge to agreement. Setting agreements, reviewing those agreements, and being accountable for them is the goal, as I have explained throughout the book. Instead of a conversation becoming a power struggle, speaking in the form of a request can pave the way for the agreement that you ultimately are striving to reach.

Turning complaints into requests can prevent a deep fissure from forming in your relationship. Instead, using requests can help you to strengthen and sustain your relationship so that it is long-lasting and has a positive quality to it.

It is the ultimate show of respect for your person when you turn your complaints into requests. That is why such action is so important. Taking the time to respectfully phrase your feelings will lessen frustration. Now, I don't mean to say that you should plan your communication to the point that you sound rigid or mechanical. It's the intention that matters, and with respect on your side, your delivery of a request instead of a complaint will land well with your person.

You have probably heard the old saying that prevention is worth a pound of cure. That's how turning complaints into requests works. Good habits begin early, like seeds sown into the ground just as winter becomes spring. Your request, spoken with consideration, can help to prevent the disagreements, shouting matches, and long, awkward silences which may be making you tired.

Word choices are important when you turn complaints into requests. When you express your displeasure, your person may hear the start of an argument. Of course, you don't want to live at odds with one another. So instead of saying "We never go out anymore" or "You are always late" (both of which can sound like nagging), avoid making an attack, accusation or assumption (AAA). With a choice of softer words, try to get buy-in at the beginning and end with the start of a beautiful agreement.

Turning complaints into requests is a learned skill, and I am here to help you to learn it. The skill takes time, practice, and patience. People with whom I work tell me the work is worth the end result.

Please don't think it's too late in the game to make the changes which I am suggesting. If your old habits are not giving you the results which you desire, why not try to do things differently? It just makes sense. Your old habits of saying "You never get it right" or "You always blame me" can evolve into requests, laced with respect, grace, and awareness of how you are being received.

To give you a better understanding, I want to share some concrete steps that you can take, which will help you to turn complaints into requests.

Number one--Turning complaints into requests requires that you better understand your person. This requires willingness and resolve from you. Even if you "don't want to hear it," try not to be dismissive or to act like you are shutting down when she speaks. If your conversation tends to go in circles, try to start a new agreement, which helps to remind her how you concur to treat one another. The simple truth is that if you both honor your agreement about something, then each of you can request to revisit the agreement instead of going off the rails or dumping complaints upon each other.

Number two—Turning complaints into requests requires that

you show a desire to connect more deeply with your person. Seek to understand how you can develop a deeper emotional connection. That connection helps you to create a foundation of good habits to navigate the roadmap when the next issue comes up.

Number three—Learn to love the other person in the way he or she experiences love. Pay attention to what your partner is showing you. Watch what they do. It's not words, but actions that you need to observe—a sign of a deeper connection developing. Tell your partner what you notice, as your connection allows you to become closer and more emotionally intimate. You've probably heard people say that they already sensed what their partners are feeling before even saying it. This type of intuition, undergirded with agreement, can prevent complaining or nagging. It's proactive. It's smart. It's going to help the two of you move to a new rhythm together by turning complaints into requests.

Number four—When you learn how to effectively design your relationship, you gain accountability. This keeps both of you honest in the understanding of why you do what you do for the relationship. When tensions flair, request that you both return to your agreement (if you have made one) about how things should go between you. A gentle reminder is far different than a complaint. A review of the new habits you promised in your agreement, or may ultimately agree to, will go a long way towards turning complaints into requests.

Number five—Remember your motivating reason for wanting to turn complaints into requests. You need and want your person to be a positive and encouraging part of your life. As you listen, your person will have the courage to believe you will do what is asked of you. Frustrations will turn into wins for both of you. You will build a strong foundation, undergirded with agreement. You and your partner can then participate in a much more fulfilling relationship when requests are mutually heard and respected.

In summary, if you do the work now in your relationship to turn complaints into requests, it will save you later, once you really fine-tune the skill. Your request, followed by negotiation, and then an agreement, are the stepping stones to getting to where you ultimately want to be. However, if you choose to complain first, it delays your time to your relationship destination. Conversely, designing and upholding your agreement demonstrates the desire to honor your relationship. Now isn't that the point of your relationship in the first place? Your requests, not your complaints, will get you there.

THE RU COACHED APPROACH

This scenario is about time management. While some people are great with time management, others find it difficult, and that difficulty can be exacerbated in relationships.

If you value time and promptness, but you are in a relationship with someone who doesn't, that can be a problem. Perhaps your relationship goes this way—you tolerate being late for events and gatherings, but this is really not okay with you.

You've probably had your fill with lateness, and you decide to complain and let your person know that you are sick and tired of walking into the middle of events. Your person knows what time you are both expected, there was ample time to prepare, and ultimately you can't reach your destination on time. You can't take one more instance. Communication is breaking down. You are angry, your tone is less than endearing. He or she is offended and sensing that you are uneasy with waiting so much.

What can you do? This conflict presents an opportunity to be smarter than the moment. It's an opportunity to create an agreement. First, you can DCIDE, as the model suggests, to introduce or to initiate a discussion with your person when you are both available and can be present to hear and be heard. What is the best time? The time when you both have nowhere to be.

I want to offer something to consider. Introduce the conversation by letting your person know that you're glad you have the opportunity to just be together without having somewhere to be, because it offers a chance to talk about concerns in the relationship and to acknowledge what you both appreciate in your relationship.

The conversation can go something like this:

You: "I'd like it if we discuss something that has been on my mind. I really want to learn your thoughts so that we can figure out our way forward together. We are often late for events and quite frankly, it's frustrating. I'd like to know how I can help you and both of us to become better with arriving on time?"

In this manner, you are including your partner with the suggestion of an agreement. As a result, the two of you have a higher probability of success and can move forward with new habits that are being set and that you execute.

COMMONLY-ASKED QUESTIONS

Q. How do I turn complaints into requests without feeling like I'm pulling teeth?

A. I can best answer this by sharing a story someone shared with me about a couple who is now divorced. The wife expressed to her wusband (lol) how much she valued communication and how very important communicating in relationships was to her. In fact, she felt that after many years of marriage, he should have known that she needed communication to feel secure and assured in their relationship. Admittedly, she said he's quiet. Getting him to talk, share, or even express himself was like pulling teeth. She grew frustrated over the years, as did he. Instead of an all or nothing approach, the couple could have had a conversation and possibly had a different outcome. We humans are innately selfish and often only focus on what we want, or desire, absent of considering what our partner wants and needs.

Do you offer what you ask? Sound familiar? Let's look deeper for a moment. If the couple had chosen to have a conversation beginning with questions and not declaratives, and talked with one another and not at one another, perhaps they would have been able to hear and be heard.

Here is something to consider: Since she knew that she desired communication and that he wasn't a big communicator, she could lead with a question. She could ask: "You have told me that you are not the best communicator and it's not really your thing, correct? Let me ask you, are you willing to meet me where you are comfortable communicating? Communication helps me to feel more connected to you and more secure with us."

If she was asking to have deep exchanges five days a week, knowing communicating is not his thing, that would be a non-starter for him. She could ask for buy-in. She could ask about what frequency of communicating is he comfortable with.

He might have said: "I'm comfortable taking some time in a day each week for us to discuss, listen, and share whatsoever is needed."

Once the negotiation on frequency of having conversational exchanges is determined, this becomes the activity which you design into and execute in the relationship. This effort will bolster a new habit, it will foster healthier relationships, and provide accountability (along with agreement) that both individuals choose to honor.

What an opportunity to learn and grow together! So, remember to start small when you want something from your person and he or she is not especially comfortable with your request. Ask for buy-in, and ask what he or she is comfortable with offering. Although this approach may seem awkward, you have everything to gain if you make the effort and remain consistent.

Q. What does it mean to undergird conversations with agreements?

A. Someone recently shared with me a story about two roommates, and one was growing exceedingly frustrated with having to ask her male cousin roommate to take the trash out. These two have a fantastic relationship. She loves him, and he loves and appreciates her for all that she does in the home which they share.

Although they are great roommates, there is one thing that frustrates her beyond measure. He sees that the trash can be overflowing and won't take the garbage out. She's asked him time and time again to do so. They've had countless conversations about it. He listens and acknowledges her concerns, yet he continues with the bad habit. So, what could she do?

Something to consider: Instead of venting frustration, use the DCIDE model--more specifically the I to introduce the concern. She could ask to speak with him to learn his thoughts about taking out the trash. In this conversation, she can also define the concern and discuss it differently than she has in the past by asking the question, are you willing to take the trash out whenever you see that it's needed?

He responds with yes. With his positive response, they can now design this task into their relationship going forward. Should she become frustrated with him for not doing what he said, she can remind him of his word and the agreement--versus having another conversation.

Making the choice to design and execute the things that matter to you into your relationships will make them stronger, because they are undergirded with agreement and accountability. That's the AA (double A), which is also a way to avoid the triple A, or the AAA (attack, accuse, assume).

Chapter Five

EMOTIONAL INTELLIGENCE (EQ) IN LOVE AND RELATIONSHIPS

When I introduce the topic of emotional intelligence (or EQ) to clients, or to groups and individuals with whom I speak, I always try to remember that while some may be familiar with EQ, others may not have come across the term.

EQ is one of those concepts that is so important for healthy relationships, but can require some work to understand well.

In this chapter, I will delve into the topic of EQ and help you to understand why EQ within the relationship which you love, can make you and the person you love great together.

EQ is commonly defined as a set of emotional and social skills that determine how well we perceive and express ourselves, develop and maintain social relationships, cope with challenges and manage stress, and make decisions. The components of EQ are relationship management, self-management, self-awareness, and social awareness.

Let's take a look at relationship management. The relationship management component of EQ is where the focus and effort are made between you and your partner to experience a deeper and more substantive connection. In order to develop your relationship management skills, it will require courage and willingness from both parties to work through the emotional vulnerabilities that can be present. It will take commitment and resolve. You may be asking yourself, "Why would I do this?" Simply, because you love your person and you desire a more fulfilling relationship.

Jeanne Segal, Ph.D, an established and well-respected therapist, book author, and expert in relationships, sheds some light on the subject. In her article, "Emotional Intelligence in Love and Relationships," she shares her insights into EQ.

EQ is a foundation of strong relationships. You will automatically sense the shifts in the dynamics of your romance and be aware of the signals for the need for action (Segal, Updated 2020).

Perhaps a signal for change in the relationships may be when complacency begins to set in. Avoid complacency by not assuming that what you are learning about your person will forever be true or what you have learned about your person is still true. We are ever-evolving. Our desires and interests may change over time and most certainly for a relationship that is well-established. Be proactive by asking questions to confirm if what you are sensing or noticing positively or constructively is correct. These are ways to demonstratively show you care. Your person matters. What matters to him or her, matters to you.

Whether you are considering a relationship or you are in a committed relationship, EQ can give us the skills we need to navigate. We don't have to choose the wrong lovers, end up in failed marriages, or let the romance seep out of our long-term relationships (Segal, Updated 2020).

In my opinion, intimacy, kindness, commitment, and caring are all within your reach, when your EQ allows you to be empathetic and to hone your ability to share emotional experiences.

Empathy and insight—these are two qualities which are manifestations of EQ. Consider designing into your relationship, periodic or regular "check-ins." Regular "check-ins" provide a runway for concerns. Introduce and discuss before concerns escalate into issues. Regular "check-ins" demonstrate the desire for you to remain connected. Moreover, those "check-ins" will provide an opportunity to ask and answer these questions for one another: "What do you need from me to feel more confident with us?"; "What areas are we strong in?"; "What areas can we improve in?"

"Check-ins" are not opportunities to blame, but to acknowledge the good and to identify areas in which you can be better together. You may choose to "check-in" bi-weekly in the beginning as the habit is forming. Once the new habit is developed, the frequency may lessen once you find your rhythm. The idea is to converse often enough, and build a positive habit that fosters confidence and comfort in your relationship.

With trust and willingness to share, you and your partner are demonstrating a high level of EQ. If your partner appears guarded or is uncomfortable sharing, remember that patience, grace and kindness will go far. If over time, sharing seems superficial, shallow, or nonexistent, then that is something that will need to be addressed as you find your way forward.

If things are working well—meaning you have both asked and answered questions for one another and you are both pleased with the responses, then keep doing what you are doing. However, I encourage you to be mindful of letting comfort and routine lull you into a false sense of relationship security. If things are going well, consider adding new habits to support your emotionally-intelligent relationship.

Segal points to the importance of actively seeking change in your relationship. Ask yourself, does your lover need something new from you? Do you need to schedule some time to re-evaluate together? Are you as happy as you used to be? (Segal, Updated 2020).

View the challenges which you encounter as opportunities, not problems. If you dwell on each adversity, challenge, or struggle as a problem, you will miss the gifts that come with them. Ask yourself, "What can I take away from this that will make me better?" Ask yourself, "What am I learning from this experience?" Ask yourself, "What am I learning about myself in this experience?" Those answers and others could provide perspective that you may not have even thought to consider. While you have high EQ, you are liberated from ruts and resignation. You can get down to resourceful problem-solving.

Segal said "respect all the feelings you have for each other." (Segal, Updated 2020). Being in love doesn't mean never feeling angry, disappointed, hurt, or jealous (Segal, Updated 2020). But how you act upon your emotions is up to you.

When an emotion develops in you, it's even more important to acknowledge where that comes from. It may not be something you are ready to talk about, but at least give your person the courtesy to know this is uncomfortable and that you need to understand what you are feeling before you can continue. It's important to use your self-management skills so that you don't do or say things that you cannot recover from.

This point takes me to another point. Values play a role in establishing standards. The self-awareness component of EQ informs your response and reaction when your values are being honored, and when they are not. Your social awareness will inform how your person responds and reacts when their values are not being honored. These data points also serve to develop and grow your relationship management skills. Your values serve as a catalyst and provide a foundation for standards to be established, acknowledged, and accepted. Boundaries provide emotional protection for your feelings and your peace.

Having a high EQ is powerful in any relationship. I would like to address new relationships here, by asking, "How do you know you are falling in love?" There is no one-size-fits-all magic answer. However, when you achieve high EQ, you can be aware of what you are feeling. You can ask yourself, "Where is this feeling of love coming from?" In other words, you can consider the source. Patiently, discover whether what you are feeling is true. A waiting period can yield a truer picture of what is going on.

EQ can also help you to know the difference between lust and love. With introspection and a thorough check on your emotions, you can determine if that powerful, intoxicating feeling is lust or love. Telling the difference may not be easy. Is your emotion based upon deep compatibility (love) or limited to physical attraction (lust)? Using the self-awareness component of EQ, you can be equipped to figure out whether you genuinely care for the person, and use your social awareness to learn whether he or she genuinely cares about you. Love is a compelling feeling rooted in compatibility.

Of course, as part of self-management, you can see whether it's time to let your guard down (we all tend to be guarded in the beginning). When you become comfortable and less vulnerable in the relationship space, you may begin to feel less self-protective. Trust yourself and honor your intuition in the moment.

Using your social awareness, you can read the relationship space you are creating. Is the person engaged with you when you speak with one another? Do you lean in or retreat? If the other person is present, you can lean in and see where it all goes. Conversely, if that person seems disinterested and aloof, you may want to consider an adjustment, perhaps a friendship, or perhaps just moving on.

THE RU COACHED APPROACH

Let's use the DCIDE model to work through a dating scenario and how to negotiate with your partner while building EQ, when love is experienced differently by each of you in the relationship.

In a recent conversation with me, a woman shared that she would share with a man that she wanted to know if he still talked with past lovers, ex-wives, or girlfriends.

I asked the woman: "Did you have an experience with someone who remained in contact with old flames?"

She responded "No". I then asked, "Why is that question important"?

She paused to think and said that one of her guy friends stays in touch with women from his past and that it always seemed suspect to her. So, she thought it would be a good question to ask.

I asked her that if she met a man who maintained contact with women whom he once dated, would she seek to learn to what extent and frequency? Or would she "throw the baby out with the bath water and give up on him"? She said she didn't know.

I asked her if it's possible that her thoughts, also known as saboteurs, are dictating her desire to ask about his past relationships versus an actual experience? Moreover, would it be worth it to introduce her concern by asking a question, and listening to hear his response about his friendships, specifically, if they are managed with respect and boundaries?

Her question could require her to discuss more to allay her concern. She said that she had not thought of it like that before.

Many times, we go into "prevent and protect" mode based on what we've heard about other's experiences or fear. Trust your intuition yourself to make good decisions. Allow answers to your questions to be validated through actions, over time. Ask yourself whether there is a cause for the thought or try to determine if it is a saboteur. Taking the time to think through your thoughts and feelings raises your EQ, specifically self-awareness.

COMMONLY-ASKED QUESTIONS

Q. What is an indication that my EQ is growing?

A: When the components of EQ—relationship management, self-management, social awareness and self-awareness—are present during an exchange and you do not allow your emotions, thoughts, or feelings to hijack the experience, you are seeing signs of growing your EQ.

For example, has anyone ever said I'd like to speak with you about something? You had no idea what about and there was no cause for concern (or so you thought). When the conversation turned into feeling critical, you felt blindsided. You had no time to prepare, you felt attacked, and perhaps, chastised.

Although you were aware of your feelings and you were angry, (self-awareness), your high EQ didn't let the person see or hear your displeasure. In that moment, you realized (social awareness) that the person was only interested in what they wanted to say and how they felt. YOU were not a consideration. Although difficult to do, you chose to display high character and to be an example of what social awareness and the ability to self-manage looks like.

Relationship management, self-management, self-awareness, and social awareness are key components of emotional intelligence in human interactions. These components can grow and mature if you put in the work, whether in a relationship that is based on love, friendship, or mutual respect.

Q: How do I negotiate with my partner and build emotional intelligence, when we experience love differently?

A: It's only natural that you and your partner experience love differently. When the way your person experiences love makes you uncomfortable, what do you do? Use the model to discuss and discover what's possible. Consider what level of engagement, attention, or effort you're willing to offer. communicate your intention to your partner. Once your intention is shared, and negotiated (if needed), the action is made into an agreement and will become a new habit for you both to work on cementing. This step is also the time to execute. Remember to execute throughout each phase of the DCIDE model.

You are creating a new practice, a new way for connecting demonstratively and intentionally. Remember to offer grace and patience to each other as the new habit is formed. The effort to initiate a discussion, communicate your intention, and make an agreement will work for you and your person, if you are willing to do the work that is required.

Author's End-of-Chapter Note

The term Emotional Intelligence, or EQ, was developed many years ago by respected and established professionals who were practicing in the fields of psychology, counseling, and therapy. Academic journal authors have explored the topic. EQ is often a component of presentations and discussions in training and educational seminars and conferences. Countless books and magazine articles feature the concept of EQ within their pages.

EQ may be new to some, yet familiar to others. Regardless of your experience or exposure to EQ, you have read and learned about its components in this chapter and will learn more in the next chapter. The EQ content in this book applies the concept to romantic relationships. Within these chapters, I share how EQ is used in my practice to develop emotional proficiency with my clients. RU Coached employs EQ as a tool to assist my clients in developing deeper, more substantive connections with their partners.

Chapter Six

IMPROVING EMOTIONAL INTELLIGENCE (EQ)

*I*n my work as a relationship coach, I find that the clients who I coach are appreciative for the insights and suggestions that I offer to them. At times, they may not be getting the outcomes which they desire in their relationships, and they may need objectivity and clarity in thinking through the issues that inevitably come up in relationships. As you know, those relationships may be new or existing.

My clients' appreciation and willingness to do the work demonstrate their trust in me to help guide them towards improved relationships. That's what relationship coaching is all about.

Improvement, especially when it relates to Emotional Intelligence (EQ), is the theme of this chapter. Why is improvement in EQ so important? Well, because such improvement suggests and demonstrates that a person is present in the relationship and aware, not only of himself or herself, but also of you.

EQ is a topic which is a little complex. It requires thought and introspection. Improving EQ is a process which requires some courage, as well. That courage will help you to take sometimes uncomfortable actions when considering the future of a relationship. Leaning on your courage allows you to pay attention to your authentic and intuitive observations about your person. This may at first feel uncomfortable, but your observations may be telling you something you should pay attention to, right from the start. Improving EQ will serve you and support you when considering relationship progress. EQ can help you to think critically about what you really want.

Just like you may have invested time and effort in your education, improving your EQ is also an investment. When learning about EQ, the overarching goal is to apply what you have learned going forward. You are going to have takeaways and results which will serve you, whether choosing a person to get to know, or strengthening an existing relationship. The investment will be worth it when you experience deeper, more fulfilling relationships.

Improving EQ is an individual choice. First and foremost, you become the best version of yourself. Your person also needs to be doing the same EQ work. Let me give you an example. If you see that your person is not emotionally-present in a conversation, you may become frustrated with the aloof attitude that you are noticing. You may self-manage and decide to revisit your feelings at a different time and place, rather than in the moment. You might check in with your partner for a time that he or she is available to talk—again, avoid AAA (attacking, accusing or assuming).

In this example, you are smarter than the moment. It is not easy, but necessary. Think about the bigger picture of your relationship success, not just your momentary frustration. I acknowledge and understand your frustration when you don't feel heard or when your feelings are ignored. However, by extending grace, patience and tolerance in those heated moments, otherwise known as self-management, you will navigate what seems to be rough waters.

Remember, relationships carry a shared responsibility. If you are self-aware, and so is your person, you will both go forward with healthy boundaries. Through self-management, you will be able to control impulsive feelings and handle your relationship in a positive manner.

Again, individual choice is paramount to help control impulsive behaviors in a healthy way. You will be able to...take initiative, follow through on commitments, and adapt to changing circumstances (Robinson, Segal, Shubin and Smith, updated 2021).

Self-awareness will show you that you know how you are feeling.

When you know what your person is feeling, and the feelings of the others you impact by your choices, you are practicing social awareness. Using your intellect and reflection which are inherent in EQ, you will understand how situations can affect your behavior, even before you take any action. Developing self-awareness and social awareness can actually prevent an unwanted conflict.

Improving your EQ is a selfless act. It is intentionally seeking to understand others' feelings. EQ goes beyond dinners and dates. Using and improving your EQ shows that you are interested in your own well-being and that of others, in good times and in bad, going well-beyond superficial actions and appearances.

Now, here is something to consider. Your EQ skills not only serve you in your personal life, but can serve you professionally, as well. Those same skills can be used in the corporate relationship space, with your mentors, colleagues and the people you supervise. Individuals become motivated and productive when you show them you care.

Work performance can improve because high emotional intelligence can help you navigate the social complexities of the workplace, lead and motivate others, and excel in your career (Robinson, Segal, Shubin and Smith, updated 2021).

Social awareness enables you to recognize and interpret the mainly non-verbal cues others are constantly using to communicate with you (Robinson, Segal, Shubin and Smith, updated 2021).

When you pay attention to the non-verbal cues around you, you are absorbing and processing information that may help you to navigate a relationship scenario that may be coming ahead. Pay attention to body language, to the tone of conversation, and to the things that are not being said. When you practice your EQ skills, you can "learn to read the room," meaning that your powers of insight and observation will tell you volumes about what is going on around you. Again, please pay attention to that.

Improving your EQ can help when you seek deeper emotional connections. At times, you may feel like you are hitting a wall with hurts or disappointments. Something may have occurred in the past, which is dredging up the water under the bridge for you.

When you are welling up with emotions, hit the pause button for a while, until you can arrive at a better place—a place of peace. You may wonder if you are willing to continue to sustain a relationship that doesn't feel satisfying. This is a useful reflection to have, but that reflection is more helpful to you when it happens during a moment of inner peace. From that place, you can be mindful of what you say to your person, so that you don't say things that the words "I am sorry" cannot fix. Using your self-management skills, you can evaluate how you are feeling. Better yet, if you and your person have an agreement in place about the situation, your chances of riding out the rough waves will be greater. After all, you both want to succeed, and even thrive.

The path to developing a mature set of EQ skills can be compared to the development of a daily work-out routine, and this is an analogy which you have already read about in this book. Let me elaborate. When you notice that your EQ needs work in order to grow the skills, you may feel like your efforts are not yet strong, similar to a work-out routine. Over time, your EQ skills, like a work-out, become significantly stronger with persistence, consistency, and maintenance. Eventually, your EQ skills become like second nature to you, just like your physical regimen. You are invested in your work-out. You are invested in your EQ skills. Then, why not make the effort? The person in the mirror (you) is in control of the choices and the outcome of the work that is needed to improve EQ.

THE RU COACHED APPROACH

This story is about a time when I observed a young, newly-married couple sharing insights about their relationship. They were discussing their top three relationship tips. Communication, having shared convictions or belief systems, and not going to bed angry with one another all made their short list.

As I listened to their relationship tips, it reminded me that, no matter the age, couples care about communication and believe it's important. Unfortunately, many of us don't know how to communicate effectively. We will acknowledge our person, but if behaviors require attention, rarely does a discussion conclude with actions that reflect the acknowledgement.

They mentioned communication as important, which prompted me to ask two questions. One, why is communication so important to couples? Two, why don't couples sometimes take the additional steps to ensure that they are communicating effectively?

There is a tremendous need to design agreement and to build the habit of accountability into our relationships. Sadly, most of us don't know how to create agreements and accountability, and consequently, we just have conversations that keep going in circles as we repeat them.

What if a couple builds in actionable steps that would mitigate frustration and strengthen the foundation of the relationship? What if there is a recognition of an opportunity to strengthen communication, share it with a partner, see the benefits, and he or she is also willing to take action? Sounds great, right?

Emotionally-intelligent communication goes far beyond the surface of "we talked about it", "he/she understood what I meant", "we both love traveling", or "we both love trying new things". It goes beyond the assumption that something that was shared was also understood. Emotionally-intelligent communication asks questions, listens for the answers, and informs choices. Emotionally-intelligent communication reveals what you feel, why you feel as you do, and how you respond when your peace is threatened.

Listening to hear and learn what a person feels, why he or she

47

feels as they do, and how he or she responds when feeling like inner peace is threatened, will develop social awareness and relationship management skills. Emotionally-intelligent communication welcomes acknowledgement, admission, and acceptance because it solidifies the foundation of the relationship. Lastly, deeper, and more substantive exchanges provide context along with insight into experiences that may have shaped the person and their perspective.

Understanding the insights which I have described at this level encourages compassion, when comments or behaviors seem out of place. Individuals and their partners can avoid AAA (attack, accuse, or assume) when they don't understand, and will be more likely to ask a question. This approach demonstratively shows caring and value for the other person.

Growing "emotionally intelligent muscles" (a phrase that I did not invent, but that is often used in coaching circles) will take time and it will take investments of effort and energy. However, the returns on these relationship investments will be exponentially-realized if the individuals mutually DCIDE to work on it!

COMMONLY-ASKED QUESTIONS

Q: What are three things you can do to improve your EQ?

A:

1. Pay attention to others. How do they respond (verbally and non-verbally) to you and to others?
2. Notice what you feel in stressful or challenging moments, and practice self-awareness.
3. Notice how you respond when you feel offended, provoked, or angry (self-management.)

The goal of these observations is to keep top-of- mind what is occurring around you and within you. Moreover, this effort promotes increased awareness and will serve as the catalyst for delivering more measured responses in challenging situations.

Q: How do I know when I should introduce a new agreement in my relationship?

A: One way to know when to introduce a new agreement is that you may be growing frustrated and want to introduce the concern before it escalates into an issue. Use the DCIDE model to introduce your frustration, and remember to avoid AAA, (attack, accuse, or assume). The goal is to discuss the issue, in order to seek to learn his or her willingness to participate in lessening your frustration. Once your frustration is acknowledged, along with a desire to work on it, be prepared to discuss and communicate more frequently, as needed.

You have experience being frustrated with your person and although he or she may understand that his or her habit annoys you, he or she may not know how to adjust. Your grace, patience, and discipline will support you because all of these qualities will be necessary to develop new habits. Introduce new habits, discuss them and communicate. Design the habits into your relationship and execute with agreement. When you DCIDE, you incorporate accountability into your new or existing relationship, which is the ultimate goal in any relationship in which the individuals are thriving!

Author's End-of-Chapter Note: The term Emotional Intelligence, or EQ, was developed many years ago by respected and established professionals who were practicing in the fields of psychology, counseling, and therapy. Academic journal authors have explored the topic. EQ is often a component of presentations and discussions in training and educational seminars and conferences. Countless books and magazine articles feature the concept of EQ within their pages.

EQ may be new to some, yet familiar to others. Regardless of your experience or exposure to EQ, you have read and learned about its components in this chapter. The EQ content in this book applies the concept to romantic relationships. Within these chapters, I share how EQ is used in my practice to develop emotional proficiency with my clients. RU Coached employs EQ as a tool to assist my clients in developing deeper, more substantive connections with their partners.

Chapter Seven

WHAT MAKES RELATIONSHIPS
SO HARD?

After helping countless individuals with relationship work, I have observed that when relationships are just getting started, they are usually not considered hard. Instead, many individuals describe the early dating stages as similar to a honeymoon phase, in which it's easy to talk, attractions are high, and the future holds much promise.

As relationships evolve, they may grow, be let go, or stay the same. The question posed in this chapter is "What Makes Relationships So Hard?" It's worth exploring how challenges come up and what individuals and their partners, or their new dating interests, can do to address the concerns.

One of the biggest challenges people in relationships can face is dealing with the ghosts of past relationships. Life challenges are common, and when something is learned from them, challenges have their value. Many times, people cannot let go of those challenges, and they can become emotional weights that they may carry forward.

When these challenges encroach on new or current relationships, then things may become hard, even though your time together once was light and enjoyable. Holding on to the past keeps you from being present in the moment. Perhaps you have not yet healed from the scars of a difficult relationship in your past. You are not alone, as many people experience traumas which may turn into triggers.

Remember, it's not a life sentence to have loved and lost. Yes, you can successfully navigate a new relationship, and even become great together. The person who hurt you before is not the person who is sitting in front of you now. Holding the new person accountable for what happened in the past is not acceptable because he or she was not a participant in your past pain.

What typically may happen in this type of scenario is that you have become so guarded, that you stop dating someone who could be great with you, if given the chance. If your relationship has become hard because your past is becoming your present, you have some choices to address it.

First, ask yourself if you are starting to really care about this person and this relationship. Then dig a little deeper with this reflective question: "Is this person who I am seeing aligned with my core values, goals, and aspirations?" The answer to this question may take some time, while you experience the budding relationship. It just comes down to what you really want and ultimately desire.

Another part of the process of navigating a relationship which seems to be turning hard is to make sure that you are transparent, honest, and self-aware. This allows you to let down your guard, communicate, and check in with the person to avoid assumptions. Otherwise, simple concerns can quickly grow into real problems that are revealing themselves after it's too late to do anything about them.

Once you identify a person with whom you believe that you are compatible, make sure that you communicate well. Then, you can make an informed decision about the future. Yes, you can start to heal from the past in order to usher in a great new future relationship, as I have witnessed with many of my clients.

Over time, as the relationship matures, things can become hard again. There are actually many other reasons why you may find that your relationship is getting hard to sustain, grow more deeply, or even feel good about. One of those reasons is that your person may stop listening to you, considering your input, or including you in decisions. Perhaps, you are starting to feel ignored or neglected when it's time to make a decision that will impact both of you.

Conversely, if you are getting to know someone, and early on, he or she wants to run things by you, then honor that. This is a measure of respect. Please also offer what you ask.

However, if decisions are unilateral, inconsiderate, or against your values, ask yourself if staying is worth it. For example, do you feel honored, or valued, or considered in the relationship? The answers to these questions will help to guide you as to whether you should continue forward, based on your own judgement and your personal choice.

New relationships tend to have similar benchmarks, or goals to reach which open the doors to a deeper, more fulfilling connection. One of the early goals is to determine whether you feel safe emotionally and whether your partner feels the same about you. Remember, trust is something which is earned. When you start to feel emotionally-safe, then the peace and stability which we all ultimately desire can begin to happen for you.

Another benchmark is knowing if your values and belief systems agree. Do you both value integrity, honesty, and commitment? When these attributes are present in the beginning, but you notice a decline, that's an indicator that the relationship is becoming hard. Once that happens, it is the perfect opportunity to introduce what you are noticing at a basic level of concern. Try not to allow this to escalate into an issue of unhappiness and frustration. A high level of social awareness will help you to frame the situation to determine what you can do to introduce the concern, rather than saying nothing at all.

Relationships can become hard when they stop growing and become stagnant. In the beginning, you may both be feeling better together than individually. Keep making the effort to be the best person for one another, and keep your relationship as the priority. Why is this important? Because you want an emotional return on your investment in one another.

Here is something to consider: Who is the person whose feedback is most meaningful in your life? The whole world can think you are great. Doesn't it mean more when the person you are with is proud of you and champions you above all else? This is a sign of a mature, supportive relationship coming from the person who matters most to you—your person.

THE RU COACHED APPROACH

The story I am now sharing is just one example of a relationship which has become hard on the couple. A young man recently reached out to me because he was a bit perplexed and frustrated with an experience which he had with a young lady who he was getting to know. He explained what was happening through his "lens". He wanted to know what I thought.

I will call the individuals in this story Josh and Mia. Josh explained that getting to know Mia was fun and exciting over the first few months. Mia even sent him a text message which said that she was really beginning to like him and that she wanted to know if he liked her in the same way. Josh responded sharply by saying "No, I don't like you. What are you talking about?"

Josh told me that he was being playful—or so he thought. Unfortunately, Mia found nothing funny about his response. She stopped texting him.

Over the next week, Mia interacted with Josh by phone and in person, just as they had been prior to her admission of interest. Josh was totally unaware about what Mia was feeling and certainly had no idea of her opinion of his sharp response to her text.

About one week or more later, they were out and Mia mentioned to Josh that she had been thinking about how to distance herself from him because he had told her that he did not like her. Josh contained himself, but was totally annoyed. He really did not understand the statement. Mia reminded Josh about his harsh text, but Josh felt that Mia knew he was joking all along. He did not mean what he had written, literally.

Josh explained that Mia should know that he liked her because of the amount of time they shared together, the things they enjoyed, and the types of conversations which they had. Rhetorically, the question that he asked himself was, "Why doesn't she know that I like her, too?"

I explained a couple of things to Josh, which I will share with you. One, I told Josh that he and Mia were still getting to know each other. It was fun and exciting, but the experience was still very new. I told Josh that he was just learning about her and vice versa. I suggested to

Josh that he remain careful not to project his thoughts and feelings. Her statement bothered him, but it could actually have been an opportunity to ask a question. No one expects the other person to be a mind reader, but acknowledging the feelings of the other person and asking him or her about those feelings is perfectly appropriate. Mia showed her feelings of courage and vulnerability when she sent that initial text, I said to Josh.

The second point which I made was that Josh did not understand why Mia continued interacting normally after the text exchange. He did not understand why she waited over a week later to say that she wanted a distance between them. I explained to Josh that two things likely occurred for her. One, the text exchange itself put her off and caused her to withdraw. Two, she developed hurt feelings about it. Although Mia said nothing, she was processing her thoughts and feelings internally before speaking.

Josh was viewing the experience through his own "lens". I suggested to Josh that he try to view the experience objectively through Mia's "lens". Her feelings were hurt, so she retreated emotionally to "sit with" what was on her mind and in her heart. Although she brought up the situation a week later, her thoughts had already formed right after she got the text from Josh.

Josh listened to my observations. I could tell that the suggestions were landing with him. He decided to send her a text response apologizing for being sharp and insensitive.

I asked Josh to consider sending her a message asking to see her in person to explain these revelations, which would mean so much more because his efforts would likely be received as sincere.

This story is an example of growing emotionally-intelligent proficiency by practicing self-awareness, self-management and relationship management skills, while demonstrating grace and compassion. Later, Josh told me that he and Mia spoke in person about everything. After the conversation, they were once again on the same page and were continuing to learn about themselves, each other, and their relationship.

COMMONLY-ASKED QUESTIONS

Q: What do I do if my partner wants to make an agreement, but I do not want to buy into that specific agreement in the first place?

A: If your partner wants to make an agreement and you don't, then consider sharing your reasons with your partner for not wanting to enter into that agreement. While the agreement is intended to hold you both accountable (which demonstrates the respect that you have for one another and for the relationship), you may want to consider an alternative solution. Consider sharing with your partner what you are willing to do or to offer. Discuss and design your new agreement, with emphasis on execution.

Q: If I sense that my partner is manipulating my emotions when I disagree, how do I handle this?

A: This situation is an opportunity to design an agreement that includes respecting individual boundaries by not using emotions to leverage your position in a disagreement. If you feel that you're being emotionally-manipulated, acknowledge what you're feeling (self-awareness). Remain measured in your delivery (self-management), while explaining (not attacking, accusing, or assuming). This step also involves relationship management. Your goal is to discuss the concern absent of emotion, even during a disagreement.

If you are both willing to implement these steps, they will certainly strengthen your EQ proficiency and your relationship. You will likely remember to keep the important things important as you move forward.

Remember that when you make an agreement, you are creating a new habit which requires that you honor it. Be open to a new way of relating to each other. However, it is easy to forget that new habit when challenges arise. Agreements—and new habits—are not meant to be rigid. Support each other in the knowledge that you are both trying to be better for each other and for the relationship. Extend each other grace, when needed. You are human and will not get it right all of the time. Eventually, you will set the routine of the new habit and it will even become second-nature to both of you. Executing new habits, discussing the bumps in the road as they happen, and building opportunities to strengthen your relationship are what it's all about.

Chapter Eight

WHAT DO I DO WHEN MY RELATIONSHIP IS IN TROUBLE?

*S*o far in this book, we have explored diverse relationship topics. I have shared the rich insight which I have developed through my experience in working with individuals and couples, who are striving to succeed in all phases of relationships.

You have read about the ins and outs of how to start, strengthen or sustain relationships, with the guidance of stories, examples, and scenarios that help to illustrate how to apply the concepts that I have been sharing with you.

Of course, even the best relationships encounter conflict, now and again. Resolving that conflict and getting to a better place is the goal. But what if the conflict which you are experiencing in your relationship makes you feel like you are hitting an obstacle which you cannot overcome? You certainly cannot do it alone. Yet, your person seems unwilling or unable to mirror your concerns, much less to do anything about them. After all, improving your relationship requires participation from your significant other, no matter what the impasse is about. You also may realize that you need to offer what you ask and mirror your partner, even when he or she may not be "showing up" for you in that way.

This situation raises the question: "What do I do when my

relationship is in trouble?" I believe that many people face this crossroad. They may want a better outcome, but they don't know how to achieve it.

When faced with this question, here is something for you to consider. Take a look at how you manage the relationship, in other words, the EQ component which we call relationship management.

I suggest that when managing potential trouble spots in your relationship, you first ask yourself a question: "Am I holding on to experiences or hurts, either from my current or past relationship?" After you give this some thought, you may realize that you could be harboring anger and frustration, or even some disappointments. Give yourself time because you may not be ready to talk yet. You may be trying to work through these feelings, as you practice self-management. Hopefully, your partner may ask how he or she can assist, given that your partner should be concerned about you and your emotional well-being.

As communication about the relationship concerns may begin to unfold, remember that becoming triggered can impact how well the communication goes. Is your body language changing? Has your tone and pitch changed because something that was said did not sit well with you? Your self-awareness is now more important than ever. Be honest about the change in you, as he or she may have noticed a difference in you.

Triggers and old habits need to be managed as you are going through bumps in the road. Part of knowing what to do when your relationship is in trouble is being open to trying something different. This requires courage, as I have mentioned before, to face what needs changing. Remember, you can only account for your own role in your relationship. Instead of defaulting to your feelings about past experiences, consider why you feel this way in the here and now. Is this mindset a saboteur which is creeping up to defeat you?

You may not have thought of conflict as an opportunity to be better. Conflict is not necessarily about battling someone. The opportunity which conflict presents can be about taking a look at where things went wrong and how you may have arrived at the point of impasse. The relationship may have started out great and been fun in the beginning. Has the novelty worn off, have you both stopped paying attention, and have you started making assumptions? Suddenly, your thoughts, feelings, and observations are no longer landing with the person who used to act like you were the only person in the room, when together.

When conflict is not perceived as threatening or punishing, you can be safe in your relationship. Try to maintain that trust as you seek to resolve the conflict. Ask questions of the one you are starting to love or continue to love, and avoid AAA (attacking, accusing, assuming). Stay true to your character, keep your word, and let honesty be your guide. You and your partner deserve to work things out in this way.

If the communication starts turning negative and unproductive, try not to retaliate or reciprocate in kind. Breathe. Pause. Make a choice. If you are clear about your values, and understand your values, lean upon them to keep things from deteriorating further. Remember, you decided to pair and partner with someone who wants the same things as you. Be thoughtful and intentional as you communicate when you think a problem may be starting, because it's never too early to discuss it.

In the midst of conflict, strive to maintain your higher self and a productive way of communicating. Try not to do or say something that saying "sorry" won't fix later on. In the midst of conflict, manage how you talk by being self-aware. Be self-aware first, because that is the priority. Then, speak carefully. This is hard to do, and not always possible. We are all human. All we can do is strive.

At times, you may grow weary with trouble that is brewing in your relationship. If you love your person and love your relationship, it may be worthwhile to seek healing. Return to the agreements you have in place, or discuss how those agreements can be created. Design a foundation that supports the stability of your relationship, to mitigate repeating the same problems or behaviors. Remember to leave room for negotiation, once you both determine that your relationship is worth the work that can lead you to the outcome you desire.

Here is something else to consider. When I hear the question, "What do I do when my relationship is in trouble?", I think that maybe a different question can be posed. The different question sounds something like this: "What do WE do when our relationship is in trouble?" Changing the "I" to "We" in this question is important because a relationship cannot be salvaged or repaired alone, as I have already mentioned. Change requires effort, energy and resolve from two people. However, you might invest effort, energy, and resolve only to realize that it's best if you part ways—or decide to let go. If this is your reality, perhaps a way to look at it is that you did not expend too much more time to arrive at this conclusion. Be grateful that you did not continue together for much longer.

Should you decide to work things out and stay, be willing to be transparent about your feelings. Allow your instincts and observations to inform your response, or to prompt questions when you do not understand. Refrain from dismissing each other.

Once you have identified areas that can be strengthened, think about what new habits would support strengthening the relationship. Discuss your ideas and be flexible as you listen. Then, begin the negotiation which leads to the agreement that gets designed into your relationship.

Remember, this exercise provides accountability and honors what you agreed to. It further demonstrates respect for each other and your relationship. Your challenges are opportunities to strengthen areas of the relationship that, unfortunately, may have started to weaken.

The story in the next RU Coached Approach section illustrates these concepts in more detail.

THE RU COACHED APPROACH

I recently considered a story about a hypothetical couple who had grown frustrated with their relationship. Let's call them Matt and Ashley. In the beginning of their relationship, it was fun, adventurous and exciting...until it wasn't. As the newness of getting to know each other waned and the two became established in their relationship, complacency crept in. The relationship that they each loved and which created so much joy was no longer fun, adventurous, or exciting.

Matt and Ashley were growing apart. They both noticed it. They talked about what they were noticing, but neither knew what to do. They found that they had settled into a routine. They had become bored, withdrawn, or distracted by the allure of someone new.

Although they had grown despondent, fortunately, they both wanted to stay in the relationship. Matt and Ashley needed to pivot from talking to taking actions consistent with their beliefs and with their willingness to engage.

Matt and Ashley wanted to strengthen their relationship. Had they known about the DCIDE model, it would have been the perfect tool to help them to re-establish the connection which they once shared. That's because the DCIDE model promotes focused effort and teaches purposeful communication, while demonstrating compassion and understanding.

When a couple chooses to implement the model, the individuals can expect a deeper connection and a relationship that continually evolves. In short, people who develop relationship management skills are well-served in the romantic relationship space, and in all relationships which they choose.

In this hypothetical scenario, what Matt and Ashley needed to do was to identify what is important to each of them in terms of their relationship. They needed to ask each other, "Are there areas of importance which we have in common?"

It's no guarantee that what is important to Matt is important to Ashley, in a mutual way. If those areas of importance are shared, then this may set the stage for them to continue their relationship.

Was the relationship fun, adventurous, and exciting because they liked to do the same things, or laughed at each other's jokes, or discovered that their values were the same so that they could relax in each other's presence? Matt and Ashley needed to arrive at the answers and get back to what first drew them together. They needed to return to creating a foundation to build upon.

As part of this exercise, Matt and Ashley needed to design what they agree on. Perhaps they value daily conversation. Perhaps they both work hard and play hard, which helps them to create balance in life. Do they both value family time? If those areas of importance differ in some ways, do Matt and Ashley extend their support to one another for those important things. Do they show up for each other and are they willing to participate in each other's priorities? The answers to these questions could likely steer them in a new direction—whether to reconnect or to disconnect altogether.

COMMONLY-ASKED QUESTIONS

Q: What are the biggest signs that a relationship is starting to enter the trouble zone?

A.

- Your partner has become distant, barely speaking to you
- Your partner is unwilling to discuss important issues, or is short in giving responses
- He or she is not willing to share time with you like before
- He or she doesn't care anymore about the activities that were once the staple of your relationship, whether a weekly dinner or other planned event which served as your signature date night
- Your partner is on the cell phone more than he or she is talking to you when you have set aside time for each other

Q. What if one person wants to let go and the other person does not?

A. The answer to this question is not popular, but it is honest. We cannot make someone choose us or stay with us. Choosing to remain in a relationship is voluntary, not mandatory. When someone you want or desire no longer wants or desires you, all that any of us can do is to respect that choice, to ultimately let go, and to seek peace.

Chapter Nine

HOW DID I MISS THAT?

*W*hen it comes to relationships, whether they are new or existing, an important question about where a relationship is headed seems to be: "Will our love last or are we letting go?" So far, this book has provided lessons about how to sustain and grow relationships, with useful information and insights that can help your love to last, if you love your person and you love your relationship.

However, there may be times when the best course of action is to let go. Whether you are letting love last (sustaining a relationship), or letting love go (ending a relationship), both outcomes require careful thought and introspection.

Now, there is not a one-size-fits-all approach to this choice. I am not necessarily advocating letting go of a relationship. That decision is up to the two people involved. I am simply providing guidance and suggestions that may help you to understand what is happening, why, and what to do next.

The topic of this chapter is called "How Did I Miss That?" The reason that I am addressing this topic is because there can be signs and signals early in a relationship that something is not going well. I want to discuss social cues because learning to read them can determine where the relationship goes next.

What are social cues? They are verbal or non-verbal cues that are shared through facial expressions, body language, and tone of voice, for example. Social cues influence how others respond to you. Through your social cues, you may be communicating unintentionally how you truly feel, and this speaks volumes.

Most likely, you can tell when someone is open to you through their social cues. These expressions of feelings are not always obvious, and may require you to use your perception and observation skills. They are important clues in what is going on between two people, and social cues should not be ignored. Instead, they should get your attention so that you can ask questions about how the other person is feeling, acknowledge those feelings, and ultimately make an adjustment, if you want to make that kind of investment of time and effort. I encourage you to pay attention and be aware of what social cues are telling you, which words alone cannot express.

Social cues which indicate interest include when the other person leans into the conversation, maintains eye contact, and seems to mirror your rhythm and cadence throughout a conversation. However, it's important to check in. You can ask a question like: "I have noticed that you seem to be enjoying our time together. Do you agree?" Remember, you are being sincere, communicative, and not making any assumptions. You would just like to know if your perceptions are similar to those of the other person. Take your time to really pay attention to what you perceive in order to know whether you want to pursue a relationship, and whether the same feelings are shared.

Reading social cues can also help you to know when a person is not really feeling open to you, and even when he or she is not feeling a connection at all. Let's look at an example which sheds more light on the topic. Imagine that you are starting to have romantic feelings towards a person whom you are just getting to know. However, that person doesn't seem to be interested in you romantically. Perhaps, he or she is feeling more of a friendship or a meeting of the minds through commonly-held interests. You may feel more than just a liking towards him or her, whereas your companion is feeling more platonic about the relationship.

How do you know the difference, especially if nothing is really being said? Responses to you initiating ideas can give you a sense of what is happening. Do you volunteer ideas about things to do together, but she or he seems evasive? Do you offer to spend more time with each other, or give out plenty of compliments, but he or she does not seem flattered? Are your efforts being reciprocated or is the other person not really responding to you? These are important social cues that you may be observing, so trust your gut intuition and don't dismiss them.

Eventually, if your efforts are not being received as well as you would like, and your suggestions are not landing well, it may be time to face the truth of the situation: that person may not be feeling the same as you are, and may actually be feeling the opposite of what you feel. It's not just about how much you like the person sitting at the other end of the dinner table.

No one likes rejection. If you feel rejected, here is something to consider. Please look at where you are in the process. By that I mean, have you just met one another, or have you shared significant amounts of time? If you just met, and you are really into the person, time will show you if there is a future.

However, if your relationship seems stalled, lacking in similar values, hurtful, or just preoccupies you, ask yourself if this is worth of continuing. The social cue could be as simple as when you reach out for his or her hand, the person pulls away and looks in the other direction. Such body language epitomizes the very social cue that deserves your attention and can express more truth than words.

There are times when the decision to let go is actually something about which to feel grateful. Why? Because you can feel grateful that you did not invest more time in a dating situation that wasn't for you. Remember that you deserve to have no regrets, and that your emotions will not always be causing you to feel so badly hurt, over time. This is easier said than done, especially if the relationship was a committed one.

If you missed the social cues that led up to letting go, don't second-guess yourself about it. This can be a learning opportunity to make you and your next partner become successful. This can be a new chapter and a chance to open a new door to companionship, love, or possibly, even starting a relationship with that person who is for you. You can reflect, heal, and even extend grace as you evolve into the person who you will become.

Sometimes social cues are not negative. Instead, they can be caring, compassionate and kind. Yet no matter how good you feel as you are receiving them, remember to check in with your person regularly to talk, communicate, and confirm what you are both feeling. This is one way to let your love last, over time.

Another important point that I would like to share is to know the difference between a relationship that seems truly meaningful and one that appears to be perhaps more tentative. Sometimes you may simply be seeking a light relationship, with no strings attached, and a chance to have fun or to just hang out. So, go for it if that is what you would like from a relationship and your person is amenable. Be honest and check in with yourself and your person about whether the pace of the relationship is moving too fast.

In this chapter, we are considering how your love will last or how to let love go. We are also talking about not missing relationship signals that are important. Remember to pay attention to the energy in the relationship up front and all along the way. Maintaining attention on social cues keeps you current and less likely to be blindsided.

Sometimes new cues show up over time because when people become comfortable, they may not be as proactive in communication. Then, one person may become irritated, or hurt, and may not have the courage to say something. So, he or she starts refraining from eye contact or sending out uncomfortable social signals.

You may wonder what is going on because you may feel like you have been kind in the relationship. Now, you may feel confused. You deserve a conversation from your person, whether the subject is difficult or not. You have the right to expect an explanation. Remember, that you are worth the effort.

Try to avoid settling and sweeping things under the rug. Have the courage to bring up your concerns and to expect the same in return. It's important to be proactive and to not let your concerns escalate into a major issue. Letting problems fester does you and the other person a disservice.

However, once you make your concerns known, if you are greeted with defensive body language, shutting down, or gaslighting, you may be at a point in your journey of entering a crossroads. You may be asking yourself, "Do I consider letting go?" You may be disappointed or hurt, but your time and attention are precious. Things do not generally get better on their own without buy-in from your person. You won't get back the time you are putting into a relationship that simply is not working. Deciding to let go takes courage, and that courage will serve you well in relationships which you pursue in the future.

Finally, the question posed in this chapter, "How Did I Miss That?" begs another important question: "Did I pay attention to the red flags at the beginning or lose sight of them along the way?" The reason that I bring up this second question is that you ultimately have to own what is happening in your relationship. What social cues have you been sending to the other person? Have you used a harsh tone? Did you look at your phone instead of at your person? Were you short with responses, or gave no responses at all? Perhaps you said something objectionable, and did not even realize it.

Self-awareness is necessary for both people in the relationship because relationships are a shared responsibility. They are a mutual endeavor, whether they take the form of "careful courting," (as one of my video presentation viewers said), or complete passion. If you respect the social cues which you are getting all along the way, the action of either letting love last or letting go will ultimately come as no surprise to you. You can make your decision with the peace of knowing that you trusted your intuition when words were not expressed, but when the actions of the other person were loud and clear.

THE RU COACHED APPROACH

There are many important reasons that you can "miss" what's right in front of you, and still wonder "How Did I Miss That?" I'd like to share a few examples here.

One of the ways that you might miss social cues is by not reading a person's body language or by not listening to the tone and pitch of someone's voice. By not asking questions, you might naturally assume that you know what a person is thinking or feeling. Such a lack of awareness could cause you to mistake someone's politeness or kindness for interest. Spare yourself potential embarrassment or spare the other person from being in an uncomfortable position. Choose an appropriate time to ask a question in order to learn if their interest matches yours.

Let's now consider a scenario that explains a "How Did I Miss That?" moment. For instance, if you meet someone who says that he or she values consistency (being consistent), you might assume that you know what being consistent means. Instead of assuming, ask the question: "What does being consistent mean to you?" Let the answer inform your response or your next question. You are aware of your thoughts on the meaning of the phrase, but that doesn't mean that your two definitions match.

Another example can happen in an existing and possibly long-standing relationship or friendship, in which the other person has been a key part of your life. In this scenario, one person harbors resentment toward the other person due to envy or jealousy. Although it's uncomfortable to acknowledge and even discuss what you notice, speaking openly can be a worthwhile endeavor if you value the person and the relationship.

While attempting to discuss your concerns, your effort may be countered with an attempt to respond to you dismissively or to gaslight you. The behavior can be subtle, it may show up as being teased about your appearance, clothing, presentation, or speech. Although the response bothers you, you don't give it much thought because you don't take the comments seriously. Perhaps, you don't believe for a moment that the person (who you value) would intentionally hurt you.

Sadly, it is not until much later that you realize that the person doesn't value you or the relationship. When reality lands on you, it can be devastating. You replay in your mind the body of work that is your relationship and the experiences which you have both shared. It takes time to process all of this.

There are two key takeaways from this scenario. One, be grateful that you now know what's been there all along and that you can "course-correct." Secondly, your goal is to learn and grow from the experience, not to wallow in wonder. This type of emotional experience is common and it can cause you to question yourself and everything that you thought you knew. Don't be surprised if you find yourself asking "How Did I Miss That?" More importantly, don't be surprised if you now have a collection of tools in your emotional toolbox that will keep you from missing such cues in your next relationship.

These scenarios come from my relationship coaching experience, and I can't wait to connect with more of you who can relate to these examples and who want help to get back on track.

COMMONLY-ASKED QUESTIONS

Q. In the beginning of a relationship, two people may be in sync mentally and emotionally. What causes the disconnect that makes people ask themselves, "How Did I Miss That?"

A. Familiarity can settle in over time, and the novelty of a new relationship can dissipate. Individuals can become somewhat lethargic in their relationship efforts, when they were once attuned to one another. Consequently, the relationship suffers. Then, inevitably, the relationship has a disconnect.

So, what do you do to avoid this dilemma? Intentionally try to remember what you did together in the beginning when things were fun and exciting. Ask your person what changes he or she would like to see. Ask him or her about the things that bring enjoyment. Tactfully confront the issue, by saying something like: "Have we slipped into starting to take each other for granted, and if so, what can we do about it?"

If you don't want to ask these questions, you will most likely find yourself asking, "How Did I Miss That?", which is a question that might be too hard to resolve at this late stage in the game.

Q. How do you repair a relationship in which a very important issue or problem just blindsided one of you?

A. The answer to this question begins with forgiveness, grace, and patience. These gifts are necessary as the offended person processes and navigates being blindsided.

Additionally, compassion and understanding should be demonstrated by both parties. Reparation continues through acknowledging the issue and its impact. When this level of clarity is achieved, the next set of questions that will require answers include the following:

- Do you want to repair our relationship damage?
- Do I want to repair our damage?
- What steps can be taken towards healing?
- Are we both willing to DCIDE?
- If so, how can we support each other while working through the residual effects of being blindsided?

Chapter Ten

THE REBOUND RELATIONSHIP

When a relationship is born between two individuals whose past relationships have not worked out, they may be seeking a fresh start. Yet, there are times when a promising relationship may give cause for pause. One individual in the relationship may find himself or herself wondering, "Is this relationship possibly a rebound relationship?"

What exactly is a rebound relationship? It involves the loss of a previous relationship, which may leave you wondering: "Is this person dating me because I am a distraction or escape from facing pain?" or "Is he or she missing what was there before and filling the void by dating me?" More questions may surface, like "Is the hurt he or she carries actually a perceived rejection from the past, which he or she is trying to resolve by dating me?"

The reason I am exploring this topic is because rebound relationships are common, and they can certainly be difficult to get out of. Sometimes the signs are there in plain sight, yet sometimes they are overlooked, unfortunately. In my opinion, rather than looking for signs that you may be in a rebound relationship, it's better to be proactive and try to avoid becoming involved in the first place.

When you meet someone new, you are starting with pleasantries which you would extend to anyone you may be meeting for the first time. You are probably not feeling deep emotional bonding yet, because it's early on. You may be a little guarded, but open to the possibilities.

Here is something to consider: If you want to choose to explore the initial attraction, pay attention and be mindful, just as you would with anyone who seems interesting to you. Sometimes, you may simply want to hang out and may not be looking for "something more". But if "something more" develops and your shared interest becomes stronger, enjoy the ride. If you are discovering one another and you learn that his or her heart has been badly broken before, lean in and listen to how he or she is feeling now. Is the person emotionally available, calm, and present with you? If you had a bad experience yourself, are you emotionally available, calm, and present, as well?

Have you been wanting to get to know someone on a deeper level? Of course, this can be an exciting process. The person could be the most interesting person, perhaps because of an attraction, an intellectual connection, or simply because it's all brand new. Regardless of what draws you, remember that at some point, it's important to share with one another, listen to one another, and to learn about one another, and that includes past relationships.

How open is he or she to sharing about past relationship experiences, lessons learned, or future relationship goals? Please do not be afraid to ask questions, in a light, conversational way. See where the conversation takes you.

If he or she seems completely closed, or dismissive, make a mental note of what you are noticing. Sometimes, the person is shy or private, which is totally understandable. Sometimes the person may not be ready to share, which is not necessarily of concern. Believe the best in people, until they give you a reason not to.

What is of concern are the red flags which you should pay attention to (Pannell, 2019): Does the person seem over-the-top interested in you, but you don't even know each other yet? (Pannell, 2019). Conversely, is it hard to determine any signs of interest at all? (Pannell, 2019). Does he or she bring up an ex-relationship and often reference the other person? (Pannell, 2019). Is the topic of the "ex" brought up randomly, and out of context? Well, he or she may still be preoccupied and deeply hurting, and not actually ready to get to know you. In addition, if you also had a bad relationship before, the other person may be asking themselves the same questions, as he or she should, with an abundance of caution.

The reason I am taking you down this path of caution is because rebound relationships can become an entanglement. How frustrating would it be if at the start, you feel like you are enjoying a great vibe and are connecting, but a few months down the road, he or she returns back to the relationship with the "ex"? That may be a surprise to you, or you may have considered this outcome to be inevitable, if you sensed that something was wrong.

Try to pepper your questions into conversations in a way that doesn't sound like an inquisition. This can feel off-putting to the listener. Allow, the answers to be validated by actions, over time. If you are interested in or curious about the person, be patient because time will tell you what you need to know as the relationship unfolds.

We have all experienced hurts and challenges in relationships. Those emotional hurts may have bruised and even damaged your heart. As you are starting the process of trying to figure out whether the other person is emotionally-viable and available, ask yourself if he or she is answering your questions with confidence. Could the person actually be a bonus to your life? Remember, as you ask your questions, listen to understand.

Not only could this approach protect you from the emotional disappointment that comes with a rebound relationship, but please also remember that your ability to be patient will serve you in this experience. Meeting someone is not always that hard. The challenge is meeting someone who you like, who likes you back, and who shares the common desire to explore the possibilities of building together.

Be patient so that the time spent together confirms your perceptions. Most of all, be prepared while in the dating space, so that your heart stays strong, and your mental outlook stays healthy. That way, you can experience the best possible outcome, whether that outcome is letting love last or letting love go.

THE RU COACHED APPROACH

In this chapter's RU Coached Approach, I want to share a story about letting go. I have changed the names of the individuals. You'll read about multiple areas of self-improvement that go well beyond just letting go.

I recently worked with Capri. She worked with me when she was just out of a relationship with Tristan, a relationship which lasted about one year. She and Tristan met and they were instantly attracted to one another. They were entering the space where emotion begins to supersede logic. By that I mean that they were developing strong feelings for one another. They passed the initial "getting-to-know-each-other" phase, and transitioned to a relationship in which their bond was more emotional than logical.

Capri asked Tristan if he was married and he said that he was divorced. Months later, she learned that he was separated and not yet divorced. (Sidebar here folks: If a man or woman tells you that they are divorced, ask them the month and year that the divorce was finalized. Secondly, check your state's publicly-available court cases to validate the claim).

At this point, Capri was already emotionally-invested with Tristan and even believed that they had a future together. She was upset, disappointed, pissed off, and angry with him and with herself (mainly herself).

One of her biggest challenges was replaying experiences from their time together. Capri was hyper-focused on Tristan's actions and less focused on how she responded to them. She didn't immediately recognize that she had a choice and that she could choose how to respond to his words, actions, or behaviors.

Capri admitted that she struggled with trust because of a past relationship trauma and that Tristan was also aware of this.

Her trauma was triggered on a few occasions while she was with Tristan. One time, they were attending a function and she witnessed him greeting a woman with a hug that seemed suspicious. There were times she would drive by his home and other places randomly, to see if he was where he had told her that he would be.

Another time while visiting Tristan, Capri smelled his bedsheets and discovered a fragrance that wasn't hers. She confronted him. Tristan attempted to use an excuse and to insert her past hurts against her in that moment. By telling her that she has trust issues and should seek therapy, he caused her to question her sanity. In short, Tristan chose gaslighting as his defense in lieu of accepting responsibility and being accountable.

I asked Capri this question: "What did your intuition say to you during those experiences? I explained to her that intuition is her ally and a form of protection. Although she did not know exactly what she was feeling or why, she could trust her intuition when it was telling her to pause or to continue.

Ladies and gentlemen, if you are ever in a relationship with someone who you don't believe you can trust, these are two questions to ask yourself: "What makes you want to stay?" and "Does this relationship add value to my life?"

In this story, there is shared culpability and there are opportunities to improve. You may have placed yourself in this story and said "not me." That's fair. Relationships are challenging and there were ample opportunities for Capri and Tristan to better self-manage themselves and their relationship. The lack of accountability, the lack of acknowledgement of "less than" treatment, and the overlooked behavior didn't serve either person.

Tristan did not protect Capri and she did not require him to. That's because boundaries were not established. Having clear boundaries informs what and who is allowed into your emotional space, and what and who is not allowed into your emotional space. Why is this important? Your personal space is your place to be protected, and is a space free of judgement, criticism, or condemnation. Only those who are willing to honor and respect your protected space are allowed. Healthy boundaries will keep out what is not good for you—emotionally and mentally. Sometimes it's okay to just let go rather than tolerating a toxic person or relationship that does not serve you, support you, or honor what you've worked so hard to establish in your life. Please remember that only you can control how you react and respond in your relationship experiences. Those reactions and responses become fortified with the presence of boundaries.

COMMONLY-ASKED QUESTIONS

Q. I want our relationship. However, my partner seems to think that she may be in a rebound relationship with me. What should I do?

A. Use the DCIDE model to introduce your concern by asking what causes her to feel that the relationship is a rebound. Allow her to answer, which will prompt your response or the next question.

Although this is challenging, try to manage your emotions and the disappointment that comes with discussing this matter. Make the effort to discuss her concerns. Confirm that she's interested in hearing yours. If she feels strongly and desires to remove herself from the relationship, please respect her choice and let her go. Although difficult to hear, process and accept, letting a relationship go frees you to heal, and to become emotionally-prepared and emotionally-available for the person and for the relationship that is for you.

Q. What is the difference between letting go of a relationship and letting go of love?

A. The two experiences are distinctly different. Letting go of a relationship where there was not love or where love no longer exists is far easier than letting go of a person who you love and letting go of that relationship.

Once romantic feelings and emotions have waned or completely dissipated, letting go is easier because there is less emotional investment. Conversely, when romantic feelings and emotions remain present, this can be emotionally, mentally, and physically devastating.

If you ever find yourself in this state of emotional hell, there are three things that I implore you to consider. One, acknowledge what you're feeling. Two, remember to extend yourself grace, as it will be even more difficult to manage what you are feeling. Three, strive to manage your feelings by resisting the urge to ask questions or by seeking closure from the person who wants out of the relationship. Realize that the answer is the answer.

How do you keep faith in your ability to love again successfully after the relationship ends? Let's face it, emotional and mental scars are real. The key is to not let those saboteurs (thoughts) condemn your belief in your ability to experience, participate, and thrive in a loving relationship. Moreover, it is vitally important to remember that the relationship that ended (which was expected to last forever) does not define you. The experience does not limit the likelihood of meeting someone who you love and who loves you back.

At the risk of oversimplification, how you think about it really matters. Your thoughts determine how you speak. How you speak determines your actions. Your actions determine your habits. Your habits determine your results. In short, if you want different outcomes—and better, more lasting relationships—don't be self-limiting. Abandon your old habits of allowing, accepting, or tolerating things which you shouldn't allow, accept, or tolerate. I empathize with anyone who fears being alone, because that fear/saboteur can be the catalyst and reason for accepting "less-than" behavior or treatment from a person. Here is something to consider: Change what you are willing to accept and stop overlooking things because you really do deserve to expect—even require—better.

ACKNOWLEDGEMENTS

- I would like to first acknowledge Jesus Christ, who has made all things possible for me.
- My mother, Gracie T. Davis, who is my heart. She is the singular person in my life who I never need to bring current with what's happening, because we speak and communicate so often. Thanks for everything, Mom!
- My brother, Kevin A. Smith. Thank you for believing in me and in the vision for RU Coached.
- Tammy McClain, also known as Tams or GA, who is my guardian angel. Thank you for sowing the seeds of becoming a relationship coach.
- The RU Coached community, comprised of individuals whom I have coached over the years and other supporters, who form what I call the RU Nation. You are believers in the RU Coached brand. I thank you! The journey is much better because you are a part of it.
- The "SIP n Chill" community, which we created during the pandemic, and was comprised of individuals who joined the conversations in our Facebook and YouTube lounges. The topics in this book will likely sound familiar to you and resonate with you.
- My close personal friends, and my extended circle of friends, who have been advocates of my efforts and endeavors from the beginning.
- Sylvia Blair, owner of Blair Copywriting and Communications, LLC, for helping me to make this book possible. Her writing and editing skills were a valuable source of assistance to take this book from the beginning to the end. I will always remember her role in this book.

REFERENCES

Segal, J. (2020). *Emotional intelligence (EQ) in love and relationships.* HelpGuide.

https://www.helpguide.org/articles/mental-health/emotional-intelligence-love-relationships.htm?pdf=26078

Robinson, L; Segal, J; Shubin, J; Smith, M. (2021). *Improving Emotional Intelligence (EQ).* HelpGuide.

https://www.helpguide.org/articles/mental-health/emotional-intelligence-eq.htm

Pannell, N. (2019). *11 Signs You Are in A Rebound Relationship.* Business Insider.

https://www.businessinsider.com/signs-youre-someones-rebound-2019-1

Printed in the United States
by Baker & Taylor Publisher Services